MEDITATIONS

Also by Ladislaus Boros
and published by Search Press

WE ARE FUTURE
GOD IS WITH US
IN TIME OF TEMPTATION
LIVING IN HOPE
MEETING GOD IN MAN
THE MOMENT OF TRUTH
PAIN AND PROVIDENCE
HIDDEN GOD

MEDITATIONS

LADISLAUS BOROS

Translated by David Smith

SEARCH PRESS
LONDON

First published in Great Britain in 1973 by
Search Press Limited
85 Gloucester Road, London SW7 4SU

Published originally under the title:
WEIHNACHTSMEDITATIONEN
© Walter-Verlag A.G. Olten 1972

English translation © Search Press Limited, 1973

Printed in Great Britain by
The Anchor Press Ltd. and bound by
Wm. Brendon & Son Ltd, both of Tiptree, Essex

ISBN 0 85532 316 7

Contents

Foreword

Christ, the God-man, really makes it possible to say Yes to life. He gave rest, comfort and peace from start to finish in his own life. When we meditate about his life we become Christians. Often we have an uncomfortable feeling that we have become blind to Christ; that we don't really know him any longer. But God's love for us appeared among us as a man. His word was: 'Come to me and I will give you rest' (Matt. 11.28). Whenever we meet this God, it is a shattering experience because he 'destroys the wisdom of the wise and thwarts the cleverness of the clever' (1 Cor. 1.19). He is a human God who can insist on our being human towards each other, with the result that he can say to us: 'Come, O blessed of my Father' (Matt. 25.34). We live as Christians by thinking about his life. His own mother's life, uncomplicated, full of care, yet happy, was made completely Christian because she 'kept all these things in her heart' (Luke 2.51).

The meditations in this book span a period of some ten years, but they all have certain things in common. In all of them, an attempt is made to understand the inner mystery of Christ's humanity. But above all I have tried to speak in them as Jesus spoke to us, simply and about simple things. The rich diversity of nature and all reality became clearly visible for the first time in the light of God's revelation. What couldn't be seen was proclaimed in parables.

He dwelt among us

He dwelt among us

No other Christian feast has penetrated so deeply into our experience as Christmas. Our main experience at that time is that God has said Yes to the world. He did not enter a strange world, but 'came to his own home' (John 1.11). This means that our world is not just our own home—and not just our world, but our whole experience and everything that happens to us: even our very own selves. All this doesn't belong to us alone. God holds sway in everything: a dynamic quality pointing to something beyond our understanding.

What is the basic content of the birth of Jesus and how should we react to it? On the one hand, it is a message of joy. On the other, it is a call to follow Jesus. We have to bear both aspects in mind if we are to think effectively as Christians about the mystery of Christmas and really to carry out the duty it imposes on us.

A message of joy
Let us consider joy first. An angel—in other words, God himself in his mediatory form—has said to us: 'I bring you good news of great joy' (Luke 2.10). There is so little joy in the world that in a sense it was necessary for an angel to come to us and call on us to live in joy. God is joy and he became man. As man, he dwelt among

us. Since that time, the Christian's task has been to radiate joy into the world.

But most of the time, our life is without lustre. It is narrow, colourless and dull. We drag on our weary way, crushed by indifference. We are overworked, lonely, sick, and separated from those we love. We often find it difficult to reconcile faith with life as we experience it.

Yet the Christmas angel spoke God's word to us in that very same life: 'I bring you good news of great joy'! In other words, anyone can be unhappy, but you mustn't. You have to make an effort to be happy. Put your worries aside at least today. Make this Christmas day, the day of joy. Ask yourself something sincerely. Ask one simple question. Suppose the angel came to us today as he did to the shepherds then and said: 'be joyful'. How would we answer him? Since the message of joy was given to men at the first Christmas, joy has become a duty for us as Christians and sadness is something that we ought to squash. But at once questions arise. How can we live in joy? Above all, how can we persevere in joy?

God emptied himself in Christ. He became man for us. By doing this, he showed us the way to joy. It is only in complete self-surrender that we can ever find the courage that is joy and happiness. Joy consists of complete self-lessness: this can be made real only when we are face to face with our fellow men. Our neighbour does not really exist for us, however, until we serve him. We experience joy in giving joy. It is quite true to say that service of our fellow men in our everyday lives is the condition of real happiness.

There is an inescapable logic in the Christmas message: we experience joy, quite simply, in self-surrender, in giving up our lives. Joy calls for renunciation. When God became man, he became detached from himself. He gave up everything for us. Our Christian lives are also made true when we give up everything in an action that is not subject to the mood of the moment. 'By this we know love, that he laid down his life for us' (1 John 3.16). We too must give up our lives for our fellow men, because our self-surrender is visible evidence of God's presence in the world and of his power over men's hearts and minds. If we feel (as we so often do) that we just can't pray any more, we should at once try to bring a little more happiness into the world. To do this is a prayer in itself, a proof that God became man.

Optimism, a 'taste for happiness', is a basic and essential aspect of being a Christian. Joy is not simply a secondary accompaniment of our Christianity. On the contrary, it determines the Christian's very being. It is the note to which all the instruments at his disposal are tuned; it is the dawn heralding the day that follows. The call to experience the birth of Jesus in a really Christian way is therefore a call to banish darkness and gloom from our lives. Darkness forms no part of the Christian's experience. It is negative and bypasses the reality of Christian life: our readiness to bear witness to our joy and to bring about a happy state of release and detachment in all the situations we meet with, even the most difficult.

This Christmas joy is a power that can change the world. It can give our fellow men a little more strength to carry on. Since God became man, we know that 'as you did it to one of the least of these my brethren, you did it to me' (Matt. 26.31–40). Christianity is there as an event wherever our fellow men are seen in their need and are accepted by us. Whatever else we may do, however useful or even sublime it may be, is of secondary importance compared with our love of our neighbour. Christ tells us, when talking about the Last Judgment in Matthew, that the love of God is shown in our love of our neighbour. This is a fundamental and unsurpassable aspect of Jesus's birth.

The life of the child who was born for us in order to lead us from a fragmentary existence to full humanity was one of undivided faithfulness in the service of others. Christ, the God-man, gave nothing but peace until the very end of his life, his death on the cross. The angel's message was an invitation to joy, but it was more than that—it was also a duty imposed on us. A man who spent years in a labour camp in Siberia once wrote: 'I looked for my God and he eluded me. I looked for my soul and I did not find it. I looked for my brother and I found all three'. This summarizes perfectly the attitude that we should have towards Jesus's birth. The angel proclaimed joy: 'I bring you good news of great joy'. To give joy throughout the whole year would transform it into Christmas.

A call to imitation

The angel's call to joy imposed a duty on us. It was also a call to imitation. We have to realize the attitude of Christmas in our own lives, which are often so dark and gloomy. When meditating on Christ's coming, we shouldn't spend our time devising theories about the nature of being a Christian. We should try instead to draw a picture of the God who 'dwelt among us': a portrait as close as possible to the reality of that God-man. What

was he really like? What was man's experience of him?
What power did he possess, that he could attract so many
followers and inspire them with the duty of imitating
him? I shall try now to describe the man in whom God's
goodness lived among us.

What strikes us at once, even after the most hasty
perusal of the gospels, is that *Jesus was a man of peace*.
His existence had a centre which was not at the mercy of
the purely chance elements in life. He was also in a
special sense detached from the world and from the things
of the world. He had a deep equanimity, a holy indifference, transcending the deadening effect of everyday habit.
He didn't bury himself in his own life or cling to himself. He wasn't enslaved by anything that was just con-
temporary or fashionable. He stayed open to everything
new, didn't try to find confirmation of his own reality,
and above all made room in his own life for everything
that he encountered. He lived, as it were, away from himself, for others.

His life was in the best sense of the word *carefree*. This
is clear from his own sayings: 'Do not be anxious about
your life.' 'My peace I give to you.' 'Do not let your
hearts be troubled or afraid.' 'I have said this to you so
that in me you may have peace.' 'Do not lay up for your-
selves treasures on earth.' 'Is not life more than food and
the body more than clothing?' 'Which of you, by being
anxious can add one cubit to his span of life?' 'Seek first
his kingdom, and all these things shall be yours as well.'
And simply: 'Do not be anxious.'

The man who spoke these words was never tense or
fanatical. Others claimed him completely, but he was
never impatient with them. He remained composed. He

let himself be led forward by his fate, which he called the will of his Father, into whose hands he 'committed his spirit', in other words, the centre of his being. His existence was quite calm, quiet and attentive. It is true to say that he had no time for himself. The whole of his life belonged to others and, in this living for others, he was never pushing or clamorous, but utterly detached from himself.

The second quality that strikes us in God made man is that *he was closely tied to the things of this earth.* He was a man who knew what earthly things are like. He took to heart not only everything that was precious and beautiful in the world, but the ordinary, drab things of daily life. His speech was full of references to the world of nature and of man's everyday experience—'the birds in the air', 'the wind and the raging waves', 'the lilies of the field', the 'vine', the 'lost sheep', the woman leavening flour with yeast, and the thief coming by night. He spoke about kings and slaves, children and beggars, soldiers, prostitutes, tenants, priests, shepherds and tradesmen. In his teaching and preaching he expressed the rich variety of nature and the whole of reality and human experience. What could not be seen was made visible and what could not be heard was made audible—in parables.

In his speech, Jesus tried to lead the world back to its original simplicity. He projected the absolute into the world of things, of everyday things. The parable flowed through his speech like blood. There is a fine balance in his way of speaking—it is both directed towards the absolute and at the same time earthly. It is simple, sometimes almost obvious, very economical, natural and unaffected. Yet it betrays deep knowledge and experience and an utter

certainty. It also shows how closely tied he was to the
world of things. Jesus's way of speaking was that of the
carpenter's son.

The third characteristic of 'God's humanity' is possibly
this—Jesus is to be found, not in the company of scholars
and intellectuals, but *among ordinary, simple people.* This
man, who was completely human because he was divinely
human, looked on such people as his brothers. He didn't
want to prove anything to them, and didn't want to say
anything basically new to them. All he aimed to do was to
reveal the shattering reality that they already knew, so that
they would come to realize that they had always known it
in their hearts. His only 'proof' was 'Truly, truly, I say to
you'. Knowledge and recognition are two distinct pro-
cesses and Jesus made it possible for people to recognize
what they had always known. There are some words which
do not require proof, simply because they are spoken in so
striking and original a way that they are quite translucent in themselves. In Christ, the word came into its
own: it was fulfilled. When he spoke, the effect was
mysterious, yet entirely simple. Words lived perfectly
when he uttered them. The beatitudes, for example,
could be understood by ordinary, simple people—the
'babes' of Matthew's gospel—yet their meaning remained
hidden from the 'wise and the understanding'. As a
result, they were understood by only a handful of people,
many of whom neither expected nor even wanted Jesus's
words to be fulfilled. He therefore remained a lonely
figure.

This is perhaps the most shattering aspect of Christ:
that he was *hidden.* His intention was to remain name-
less. The loneliness of fulfilment was revealed in his life,

the solitude that we associate with mountain heights and the depths of the ocean. Man's existence is fragmentary and fleeting. The man who, like Jesus, aims to experience the oneness of life must be prepared to remain alone. In this way, he will be able to concentrate on the unity of being. Jesus was alone as he grew up, alone in his temptation in the wilderness and alone at the most important moments of his life, in all of his most decisive actions. He moved among us like a star, suddenly and unexpectedly crossing the sky of our experience and only noticed by those who chanced to look up. His origin was unknown. He appeared, his light shone suddenly, briefly and powerfully, and he returned to the unknown. He was 'a light that the darkness could not overcome' or, to use the other meaning of the Greek verb (and John was probably playing on both meanings), 'light that the darkness could not understand'. He was surrounded by people who didn't understand him. Laws and prohibitions, customs and traditions were quoted in argument against him and even his own mother reproached him. Everyone criticized him in one way or another, although perhaps not openly, for being different.

All the same, despite his loneliness, Jesus lived—as it were—'*easily*' on earth. He knew that his essential being would not be understood by most people, that it was inaccessible to them, but he did not worry about this, because he realized that perfect speech is usually not heard and perfect being is not perceived. He did not promise that we would *find* anything through him. He taught us, on the contrary, to *seek*, to look for the name that cannot be named. 'Seek', 'look for'—the notion has a central position in all that he said. It is not possible to understand his life according to the principles of our own petty selfishness. He was possessed by a holy and vital youthfulness. Nothing that was hard, inflexible or closed had any place in his life. Because his spirit was youthful and open, he was able to teach us how to be young, to be born again, to be transformed and become fresh and happy, holy in the fullest sense.

Jesus insisted that the man who did not give himself up completely could not receive the kingdom. He was our guide to a new life, the beginning of a new creation and the foundation of a new world. He called on the Christian to become a 'new man', to be 'born again', to renew himself every day, to look forward in hope to a 'new heaven and a new earth', to sing a 'new song', and altogether to be a radically transformed person. This totally new being lived in him and what he achieved was the fruit of the concentrated oneness of his being. He came 'so that my own joy may be in you and your joy may be full' and 'I have come so that they may have life and have it abundantly'.

This 'central' man was also *everybody's friend*. He reconciled and united men and made them whole. He insisted that we should not hate each other, that we should not repay evil with evil, that we should love even our enemies. Above all, he wanted to inspire everyone with hope, so that we should have the confidence to renew ourselves and live a genuine life of freedom. His rule was true and he brought everyone into his oneness without doing violence to anyone. He made it possible for us to be happy of our own accord by letting himself be disfigured by the suffering of us all. In doing this, he showed himself as a king, whose rule was true. He was united with everyone in love and mercy. 'Come to me,' he said, 'all you who labour and are heavy laden, and I will give you rest.'

He was 'the light of the world', the 'true light that enlightens every man'. He gladly accepted publicans and sinners and told everyone that he did not condemn them. He defended sinners in the presence of so-called just men and protected children from adults. His sympathy for those he met was so great that he often wept. Men imitated him because they saw that their negligence grieved him. He was aware of the need of everyone he encountered. He perceived the need of the poor widow and gave her only son back to her. He sensed the need of the sick woman who touched the fringe of his cloak in the crowd, and cured her. He knew the need of his friend who had denied him three times and whom he looked at and forgave. His respect for every creature was unlimited, and the attention that he gave to every living being was most tender. Christ's way was the way of unlimited life lived most tenderly.

He lived a fully human life, including all the ordinary, tiring, repetitive and everyday experience of any human being. He fully accepted frustrations and temptations and, without sinning, experienced the narrow restrictions of the human condition. He was a friend of the oppressed. He also enjoyed the little things of life: a good meal, a tasty drink, a pleasant walk, a sincere friendship. When he met his fellow men, he did not dazzle them with appearances. When he suffered, he did not suffer ostentatiously, but we know that he cried out, sweated blood and felt drained and forsaken.

In this way, Christ ruled in men's lives and the king-

dom of God came into being as something that could only
be established by him. He threw light on the basic reality
of man's existence and, as the one whose rule was true,
he bore others' pain and suffering, exposing himself to
all their needs. He set up his own inner truth in a world
in which truth was absent, indifference prevailed, the
struggle for power had captured men's hearts and con-
fusion reigned. In this world, he had, as it were, to ex-
tinguish himself and to listen to the truth of things that
was, in his case, independent of every claim to power. He
had to rid himself of all illusion and keep his gaze fixed
calmly, clearly and objectively on what was essential and
above all thrust aside everything in him that might prevent him from throwing light on the holiness and purity
of man's being.

This attitude called for humility, renunciation,
sacrifice and a complete forgetfulness of self. The man
who tries to do this has to shift the weight of his being
outside himself. The whole world, unimpaired, bright
and holy, is made present in a person who is really looking for the truth. Untruthfulness, on the other hand,
destroys the power of man's being. It changes the world
into a stage where man dissimulates in a parade of his own
selfishness, an arena where every instinct to dominate is
given full play. In such a world, the straight is made
crooked. In a world of lies, it is no longer worth the effort
to be committed to anything, to say Yes to anything with
total conviction or to say No with equal determination.
Freedom, humility, human togetherness, love and anger
are all made impossible in such a world. What is essential
becomes inessential; what is true becomes untrue; and
what is human becomes inhuman. Jesus came to bear wit-

ness to the truth in that world, and the only possible end was crucifixion. Everyone who looks for truth has at some time or other been asked, in a tone of resignation, 'What is truth?'

When he was crucified, Jesus forgave everyone, praying to the Father, 'forgive them; for they know not what they do'. He did not try to find answers to political questions or social or philosophical problems. Instead he gave hope to a broken and abandoned wretch: 'Truly, I say to you—today you will be with me in paradise.' It did not matter to the dying Jesus that the man had not led a decent, respectable life. He was a poor criminal who had been tied to a cross near him and could not escape death; Jesus spoke to him as the angel spoke later to Peter in prison, telling him to get up and go. But this man could not just get up and go. All the same, he obeyed and went where his nailed feet took him—to the realm of the one who is completely different. Anyone who has ever thought about a radical change in the whole of man's existence must know, after reflecting about Jesus's death, how this is accomplished: by forgiveness and by giving hope to those who seem to have no more hope.

It would be unbearable to think of Jesus having no one to help him at the end of his life, but there was someone with him who understood this complete purity and sincerity that he embodied and who could accept it entirely. That was a simple woman, his mother. Jesus found a last refuge in her, his original home. There had to be someone who was not treacherous or a coward, who did not deny the life of truth, who was not dishonest and who did not dissimulate: someone who could accept him completely.

He said very little to her from the cross. There was no need for them to say much to each other, but the few awkward words that Christ spoke to his mother and to us just before his death will live for ever in men's minds. They call on us not to seek power, not to manipulate or misuse each other, not to lie and not to distort the truth. They make us conscious of our duty never to betray a friend in any way, never leave our fellow men in their loneliness, never to reject those who are abandoned, always to look for the truth, and always to be aware of a person's inner attitude rather than his outward appearance. They call us, in a word, to purity. These last words which Christ spoke from the cross are utterly simple: 'Behold, your mother.'

This attitude, which Jesus acquired throughout his hard life, the attitude of his incarnation, became definitive in his resurrection and ascension. This was one of the essential aspects of the apostles' experience of his ascension: that goodness, forgiveness and love had become the ultimate norm. And now this attitude of Jesus's incarnation is something that cannot come to an end. God has given us Christ—a new beginning.

Christmas is more than just a mood. It is, above all, a task that we as Christians have to carry out in our lives. God became man and lived among us. He is a human God. He calls on us simply to be fully human. This humanity is lived in joy and in imitation. It is not easy to say which is more difficult to achieve nowadays. God wants us to live in joy and to imitate Jesus in our lives. This is the message of Christmas and its summons to us.

Feast of silence

Feast of silence

When Christmas comes, many people feel a need for silence and reflection. They want to be alone for a while and to think, even though rather vaguely, about all kinds of things that have nothing to do with their everyday life. Only very few people think very deeply at this time and even fewer consciously engage in religious meditation, and when they do so, it usually takes up only a few moments of their time. It would not be wrong to say that, for almost all of us, Christmas is thoroughly profane and that what happens to us at this time is that a strange but powerful reflective mood overcomes us. But, paradoxically enough, it is often in the secular thoughts that pre-occupy us at Christmas that the holy element comes close to us. This is simply because wherever we are open in our humanity the mystery of God is present among us. God is very close and can be found in the most obvious and simple things. He is closer to us than our own hearts. Having said this, we can now ask: what does the ordinary, simple person think about in those moments of silence?

What we usually experience above all then is a number of memories. Every one of us carries with him something that is very carefully protected from the strains and stresses of everyday life. In these times of silence that occur especially at Christmas, we recall moments during which we experienced life very intensely, times of suffering, great happiness, tender love, shy friendship or unfulfilled longing. A human face, a habitual gesture made by a long-lost friend, a colour, the shape of a countryside well known in the past—these we remember, sometimes with astonishing clarity. We like to keep such memories with us, dwell on them lovingly. We feel at home in them, because what is most precious to us is made present in them. At such times we realize that our lives contain certain unique elements, experiences of special grace and power, and that even insights that we had forgotten long ago can come to light and appear totally convincing again. In those moments of recollection, too, we see with great clarity that convictions and attitudes which can barely survive the hard experience of daily life are of the greatest value and importance.

What are these convictions that are so easily broken, yet so supremely valuable? They are that it is good to be selfless, to be sad with those who mourn, to hunger and thirst for righteousness, to be pure in heart, to be merciful and to be a peacemaker. These convictions are not something that we can proclaim from the roof-tops, but they are good to think about and we can savour their deep mystery when we are alone. Our everyday experience can equally well be shared and understood by others, but no one else can live out that fragile inner experience that is made present to us in those silent, lonely moments of recollection.

Whatever we may think about when we are in this mood of recollection, it will almost certainly point towards what is wonderful, mysterious and outside the sphere of what we can perceive with our senses. This is why the birth of Jesus has always been crowned with a halo of wonder. The Christmas stories make clear what is sensed then: that man's experience, dark and confused as it is, goes much deeper than the everyday level. His longing for wonder is an authentic part of his psychology and cannot—to the regret of many theologians and philosophers—be dismissed as pure superstition. It is something that gives him the inner strength to resist the emptiness and nothingness of his existence. The truth that underlies our longing for wonder is that it is possible for us to go beyond the world of everyday experience and reach the sphere of the unsurpassable. We are not simply at the mercy of the hopeless and often bad experiences that we have in the everyday world. These do not ultimately determine what we are and what we may become. New and unexpected things can always rise up out of our lives because there is, despite all the anxiety and unhappiness that surrounds us, a hidden source of salvation in the world that can begin to flow at any time. Something that is bright and pure and not simply superstitious or wildly enthusiastic is proclaimed in this Christmas mood. It is that, despite all the evidence that exists in the world as we know it, there is a way from darkness into light: there is a light shining in the darkness of the night.

This tendency to recall the past often makes us seek the company of children at Christmas. When we are with them, we gain an insight into the mystery of childhood, but we often feel a little sad as well. What does it mean, that sadness that grips our soul when we think about our own childhood? It is above all a feeling that we have lost something quite irrevocably, the direct contact with experience that is the most striking aspect of being a child. When we were children, we could be held spellbound by things, by events and sensations, and so completely absorbed in that experience outside us that we did not glance back even fleetingly at ourselves. We were whole and undivided, and as such very close to something whole, single and undivided. At such times, it did not even occur to us to account for or justify anything. We were simply there, completely given up to that overwhelming experience with our eyes wide open.

When we recall that childhood experience, we sometimes begin to sense the real profundity of the saying which at other times seems so superficial and even sentimental—that children are angels. This does not mean that the angels are simply pretty and attractive—far from it. But angels and children are very similar in one respect—in the intensity of their being. It was precisely this that made the Austrian poet Rilke call angels 'tumults of tempestuously enraptured feeling'. It is not simply that they *experience* rapture in the burning transference of their whole being when they are carried away—they *are* that very rapture, that being carried away, that total self-surrender and self-forgetfulness. In this way, children are often like angels, especially when they are playing. It is also precisely this that we adults long for—our lives and sometimes even our whole appearance are usually so covered and obscured by activity, worry, self-seeking and self-assertion.

Ordinary, simple people also give special attention to their womenfolk at Christmas, surrounding them with love and respecting above all their rôle as mothers, because women represent true tenderness. Tenderness is never a sign of weakness or inferiority. On the contrary, it is a readiness for love and affection which protects all that is most precious in the world and which acts with great sensitivity and restraint. Women are more directly in touch with and more deeply rooted in the mystery of life than men. They understand the confused relationships of human society more quickly and are less preoccupied with theories and concepts. They are much more concerned with life as a whole and are more intuitive.

But why is this tenderness so indispensable to life? One of the most important insights gained in recent philosophical thought is that higher, superior values often show themselves to be weak, threatened and inadequate in comparison with the lower values, those regarded as inferior. How weak human life itself was at the beginning of the evolutionary process—its origin was surrounded by accidental circumstances and it was exposed to every element of chance. How helpless man's spirit was when it began to emerge from the purely organic sphere and to achieve consciousness for the first time—seeking, hesitating and taking man further away from the warm safety of the natural basis of his life. How fragile the higher insights of man's spirits seem to be in the everyday world of today—the idea that gentleness can, for example, be stronger than violence—and how apparently unsuccessful, immature and even antiquated or backward-looking.

How lost a quiet person can seem among fluent speakers. How vulnerable beauty is in the world of useful things. How tender hope is and how uncertain and wavering it seems when compared with the other, more obvious virtues. How little room we can make, living in a world of harsh reality, for the ethics of Jesus as outlined in the Sermon on the Mount. How quickly our dreams are shattered by the hard facts of everyday existence. How ingenuous a person seems if he tries to fulfil the demands of Christian love; if, in other words, he tries to be patient and kind, is not jealous or boastful, is not 'puffed up' or rude, does not insist on having his own way, is not irritable or resentful, and puts Paul's teaching as far as he can into practice, not rejoicing at wrong, but rejoicing in the right. How strange an impression is made by the man or woman whose life is governed by such essential principles. And ultimately, how impotent God seems to be in his own creation.

In this ascent of being, from the first awakening of life to its completion, one fundamental law of the universe can be perceived. The first unfolding of man's being, the upward movement of his life and his entering the ultimate reality are part of a process in which tenderness becomes more and more tender, what is threatened becomes more threatened and what is already exposed to chance becomes more exposed. The cross is in this sense the fundamental law of all life, a law which was ultimately, fully and most sublimely realized in Christ. Woman's highest vocation is to be seized by this basic law of life, to experience it, body and soul, all the time in her own life and to go out into the world thus equipped and protect it. In this way, woman shows herself to be, *par excellence*, the one who, despite all suffering, can continue to stand patiently beneath the cross waiting for a resurrection.

In addition to remembering children and our womenfolk, we also like to give special attention to old people. We want to give them happiness and be kind to them. Old people remain tied to life by very thin and easily broken threads. They are at the very end of their resources. What are the thoughts of an old person?

How quickly the years have flown by and how strange it has all been! Has my life been a dream or was it really true? So much of what I once thought important seems of little value now. My whole life seems to have flowed away from me—decisions that I have not taken, plans that I have not carried out, experiences of beauty that I have failed to appreciate, struggles in which I have taken part, perhaps in order to try to become what I have never been, at least externally. And now I am imprisoned in what I have in fact become and can never be any different. I am just this particular person and I have become what I am now, because or perhaps in spite of all the many promises in my life. Very little remains now. I have a few periods of solitude left, moments of sincere selflessness, times spent with a loved one, a few good deeds torn, as it were, forcibly from me, a certain determination to go on living, faithfulness, the persistence of hope despite all the failures of life, a helping hand, the first experience of love. Very little. What seems important to me now is what has happened as it were incidentally to me throughout my life.

These are, I think, the typical recollections of an old person who has learnt the meaning of deprivation. Thinking like this, he experiences a tender love for everything that is done in vain, for what is wasted, superfluous and foolish in the world. He feels at one with failure and imperfection, with all those who have not succeeded in life.

He therefore possesses one of the rarest and most precious mysteries of all—forbearing patience. When we are caught up by the mood of Christmas, we can remember the tragic yet beautiful fate of old people and try to be very kind to them, to make up for our impatience and irritability in the past.

Children, womenfolk and old people are not the only ones who should be in our thoughts. We should also remember with love all those who are unsuccessful, and try to give them fresh hope. The lonely too are especially in need of our presence. Refugees, prisoners, sick people and those who have died—such people are bound to be in our minds, and their situation makes us think seriously about our own. We also think of those who are sad or unhappy, those who are full of doubt, those who no longer believe and those who cannot escape from the prison of loneliness. We should also remind ourselves of those whom we have, perhaps unintentionally, wronged, those who are hostile to us and even those people who simply do not like us. When thinking of Jesus's birth, we ought to do some good to everyone, forgive them everything and ask them to forgive us. We should be people who can offer a home to everybody.

How close to God this longing is! It is so near to the heart of our redeemer, who embraces us when we are rejected, receives the beggar, takes the one who is falling to himself and is a God of all those who stumble, who are tempted, who are outlawed and who fail. All this is very close to the God who gives his blessing to our lives, who has descended into the depths of our souls, who shook off the nocturnal shadows of death for our sake, who visits us in our loneliness and who loves the least important and the most hopeless people most tenderly of all. It is very close indeed to the God of love.

The ordinary, simple person, then, can reflect, in those few moments of silence, about all kinds of things that usually affect him at other times in only a rather superficial way. These reflections are not sublime meditations or profound thoughts. Their value, however, is to be found in the fact that they take place in a spiritual atmosphere of love and affection. They do not necessarily lead to any kind of action. All that we have to do is to dwell on them and look at life quietly, with love and without illusion. How can a person who does this be described?

He would be surprised if we were to tell him that during those quiet, reflective times he was thinking in the way that God himself thinks about us. He would never have dared to believe that God's thoughts were so simple and so obvious or that God could ever be so close to man and to all that is human. At such times, he does not ask for God at all or look for him—all that he does is to give way to the impulse of his own heart. Yet he experiences, in this mood, a God who is always near to us even if we do not seek him—'I was ready to be sought by those who did not ask for me; I was ready to be found by those who did not seek me. I said, "Here am I, here am I".' The same idea, expressed here by the prophet Isaiah (Isa. 65.1), was formulated by Paul in his astonishing elucidation of Deuteronomy 30.11–14 in his Letter to the Romans: 'Do not say in your heart, "Who will ascend into heaven?" (that is, to bring Jesus down) or "Who will descend into the abyss?" (that is, to bring Jesus up from the dead). But . . . the word is near you, on your lips and in your heart' (Rom. 10.6–7).

Jesus is not a stranger to us. He is the concentration and climax of everything that is genuine and true in our existence, of all self-surrender and of all the help we give to others. In his quiet thoughts, the ordinary, simple person senses Jesus's presence as his eternal brother and in his heart as the centre of his human activity, even if he does not consciously think of, or feels that he is a long way from Jesus.

Love

Love

It would be unthinkable if I did not include among these meditations some thoughts about the fundamental Christian attitude of love. The word 'love' has, of course, become notoriously ambiguous in recent years and it may always have been so. But, despite all the highflown things that have ever been said about it, the only people who really understand love in its essence are those who have personally experienced it. The Christian answer, then, to the question: 'What is someone leading an authentic, radical human life really like?' is simply—such a person is one who loves.

We must try to express in words at least some fragment of this human longing for love which all of us experience at some time or other in our lives. Perhaps—who knows—we may succeed in painting an authentic picture which is very close to the reality that we call love, that presence which we sense within us and which we almost take for granted, however mysterious and almost incomprehensible it may be. Love rises up, an inner necessity, almost a compulsion, from the depths of our unconscious and, as soon as we become aware of it, takes control of us completely. When we once begin to love, we can do nothing else but love. Love is a strange urge within us, so strong that it sometimes hurts us and at others can even have a catastrophic effect on our lives and those of others. It is therefore very important that we should learn how to love, how to take in hand this powerful impulse that rises up so mysteriously within us and overwhelms the whole of our being. We cannot allow it to run riot, give it free rein to go where it will, without any aim or sense of direction. We have to fashion and direct it, let it fulfil itself or even prevent it from being fulfilled. Formed and controlled in this way, love becomes a mature, authentic virtue, in other words, a practised and painfully disciplined attitude towards the world. If love is not really learnt, it may result in unmeasurable pain and suffering. This is the paradox of love—that we are bound to love and that we must at the same time learn to love through pain and adversity. Simply to let love remain at the stage of pure, uncontrolled feeling is to let it enflame us with daemonic and even destructive power.

It is advisable, then, to be very cautious of using high-flown language in speaking of love. Tender things must be handled tenderly. We should therefore approach this sublime reality of human life as something holy and of great value and, before we enter its mystery, open the door of our mind very gently and tune our thoughts delicately into it. In the history of Western spirituality, no text contains such essential truths about love as a practised Christian attitude as Chapter 13 of Paul's first Letter to the Corinthians. So important is this text that we cannot do better than to meditate about it here and to allow its message to enter our hearts. It is possibly the most concentrated and meaningful expression in the world of all that is essential in the Christian attitude!

'If I speak in the tongues of men and of angels, but

have not love, I am a noisy gong or a clanging cymbal. And if I have prophetic powers, and understand all mysteries and all knowledge, and if I have all faith, so as to remove mountains, but have not love, I am nothing. If I give away all I have, and if I deliver my body to be burned, but have not love, I gain nothing.

'Love is patient and kind; love is not jealous or boastful; it is not arrogant or rude. Love does not insist on its own way; it is not irritable or resentful; it does not rejoice at wrong, but rejoices in the right. Love bears all things, believes all things, hopes all things, endures all things.

'Love never ends; as for prophecies, they will pass away; as for tongues, they will cease; as for knowledge, it will pass away. For our knowledge is imperfect and our prophecy is imperfect; but when the perfect comes, the imperfect will pass away. When I was a child, I spoke like a child, I thought like a child, I reasoned like a child; when I became a man, I gave up childish ways. For now we see in a mirror dimly, but then face to face. Now I know in part, then I shall understand fully, even as I have been understood. So faith, hope, love abide, these three; but the greatest of these is love.' (1 Cor. 13.1–13).

This text is an astonishing mixture or succession of statements, demarcations, contrasts and interpretations. We shall consider it above all with what it has to say about man and his attitudes and thought in mind, in other words, from the anthropological and philosophical points of view, and we shall see, as we examine the text more closely, that it is impossible to speak effectively about love in any other way. What is most remarkable is that Paul makes no attempt to define love as such. There is a de-

41

marcation—in other words, he marks love off from other gifts and virtues—but no definition. He also enumerates the qualities of love and circles around them. This process reveals a very important aspect of love—that it has above all to be experienced. We have to be shattered by it. Love is a primordial experience in our lives. Its essential, original and fundamental aspect, however, always eludes our grasp and we can therefore never discuss it. The essence of love is simply given to us as an experience. This experience is first of all that:

Love is everything.

If I speak in the tongues of men and of angels, but have not love, I am a noisy gong or a clanging cymbal.

We do not need to examine in detail here what Paul was saying to the Christians at Corinth—we should rather try to discover what his own experience was. It is clear that there were people in the community there with special spiritual gifts who had reached the ultimate point of human experience and were able to express (in hesitant, stammering language, it is true) the inexpressible. The historical and psychological details of this 'speaking in tongues' are of secondary importance to us here. What is above all important, however, is the fundamental experience that, however beautifully you may speak, as beautifully as any man or even with the eloquence of an angel, if you lack love it is just 'sounding brass', empty nonsense, and you have neither done nor even experienced what really matters. Your speaking sounds good, it may even move your listeners, but what lies behind it? Nothing. Emptiness. You utter words, but the reality is not contained in them. What you say, your talk, your sermon, your lecture, may be stimulating, inspiring, very touching and excellent in many ways, but you yourself are not behind it and so it lacks meaning and content and ultimately leaves people sad. You are only looking for yourself and trying to make an impression.

For Paul, love is first and foremost service of others: action. If you have never loved, how can you dare to speak about the reality of love? You will simply be presenting a favourable picture of yourself in words that will quickly be lost. First prove that you value the other person more than your own life and that you will defend him from the cares of the world and the injuries it can inflict. Give him shelter. Protect him, if necessary against himself. Fight for him, give him life, let him grow and expand inwardly. Talking about love is, for Paul, empty and hollow without the experience and action of love. We have first to prove in our lives that our words are sincere. It is very easy to deceive other people. Even very substantial talking is of no use at all if love is absent from it. Love communicates itself in silence, by simply being and remaining there, giving help and support. Anyone can utter fine words—it depends on his sensitivity to language and his gift for speaking. The true language of love, however, sounds quite different. What is heard in it is not emotion or even intelligent reasoning, but self-surrender.

And if I have prophetic powers, and understand all mysteries and all knowledge, and if I have all faith, so as to remove mountains, but have not love, I am nothing.

Another, even more striking demarcation. A prophet is a person who can interpret the events of this world in the light of God's grace. A man can 'understand mysteries' when he is able to remain in the presence of the inexplicable and grasp it with the whole strength of his being, penetrating ever more profoundly into the hidden truth at its centre. A man 'has faith' when, perhaps despite inner doubts, he exposes himself to a reality which cannot be constructed from the material of this world. He has faith when he allows himself to be claimed in the depths of his being by the absolute which he cannot explain. He has faith when the inner power that comes from his being claimed in this way enables him from time to time to do things which amaze the world and which can, in other words, 'move mountains'. These three qualities, prophecy, knowledge and faith, together provide a very impressive picture of the deep reality of human life, that of prophetic, knowing and believing existence. In the anthropological sense, it is a picture of man's fundamental and all-embracing dynamism, his essential reality. Yet even to this, Paul says, prophecy, knowledge and faith are very important, beautiful and indeed indispensable, but they are not the most essential or the ultimate human reality. That reality is love.

What, then, is that love to which Paul gives such priority? The more firmly he marks love off from the other spiritual gifts, the more distinctly it can be seen that if we have not love, we are nothing.

If I give away all I have, and if I deliver my body to be burned, but have not love, I gain nothing.

Karl Barth said: 'There is a love which is without love, a self-surrender which is not surrender, a paroxysm of self-love which has the external appearance of an authentic love of God and our brother, the love which will go to the ultimate limits of self-surrender, but which is in reality not at all concerned with God and our brother . . . Only love itself counts; no acts of love as such, not even the greatest. These can also be done without love and they are then meaningless. Even worse—they are often done against God and our brother.'

Love has previously been described as action, but here selflessness is added as an essential element of love. Although it is also possible to look for oneself in 'love', it is equally possible to lose that love in unselfish activity. There is a strange and little recognized quality of love which can best be described as not knowing about oneself, not regarding oneself, or as an absence of intention. A man can give up everything, he can even go so far as to lay down his life, but if this is not done quite gratuitously it is nothing.

This brings us to the ultimate limit of what can be expressed by language. We can perhaps say that love is simply as the psalmist said: 'I have become a beast of burden before thy face'. This not knowing about oneself, this pure self-surrender, this wanting nothing from the other person, this acceptance of being a stranger—all this is love. Without this fundamental selflessness, we are nothing, however many acts of love we may perform. If we are not totally selfless, we do not really love—all that we are doing is looking for ourselves. Anyone who has ever loved knows that it is possible to put another person in the wrong even by being good to him, to do him an injury by giving oneself completely to him. If we remain attached to ourselves while loving, it is not love at all.

The underlying thought of this astonishing text is inexorable, but it is ultimately consoling, because it reveals to us the real dimensions of our own humanity. Strangely enough, however, Paul's teaching about love now abruptly follows a different and unexpected direction. He describes, first positively and then negatively, the qualities of this essential human attitude of love, although he had previously hinted that he could not speak about it at all.

The qualities of love

Paul's description of love is, of course, very fragmentary. One has the impression that he has himself experienced love in its essence and that he cannot speak about it precisely for this reason. His ideas in this passage come not so much from his intellect as from his heart, so that they have a strange logic that can only be understood by the heart. This deep experience of love enables him to release, as it were, fragments of intuitive knowledge, each one of which goes to the heart of the matter.

Love is patient. This description of love begins with an apparently insignificant but in fact living quality— patience. It is this quality that makes it possible for a person to persevere with someone else for a long time, even until death : for him to bear with that other person, not in indifference and neglect, but in creative faithfulness. Patience is the courage to bear with others, to help them to bear their own existence. It is the courage to go on in time and to give oneself to others perhaps in new and different ways. It is the courage not to cut through the thread of love and to show, by our presence, that the other person can rely on us in all the different situations of life, that we will remain with him. Without this courage to give ourselves faithfully and patiently for a long time, the proximity of other people can be a form of hell.

The Christian whose aim is to love authentically and thus to became fully and authentically a human being has to educate himself to be faithful to the point of being ready to give up everything. He must never capitulate, but persist to the end. His life's task is to overcome disagreements, however long this may take, and patiently to learn how to control the fluctuating impulse of love. Seen in this way, love can find its true expression in our being unconditionally present for other people for ever.

Love is kind; love is not jealous or boastful. This quiet, humble and long-suffering patience, which reveals itself as a complete openness to others in all the situations of life, has to be accompanied by kindness, a friendliness, a peaceful serenity in being together with others—a togetherness that is always threatened by nervous agitation and a loss of peace—a silent acceptance of others' failings, their fickleness, their inner restlessness and their physical and spiritual imperfections and a tender, considerate and sympathetic forbearance. A love that is kind will moreover not be jealous. In other words, the person who loves patiently and kindly will not seek recognition. He will not set himself against other people, try to put them in the wrong or list their faults and failures. He will not allow himself to be affected by a bitter and unhealthy animosity towards his fellow men which would eventually undermine his whole existence and which is ultimately only a form of self-righteousness.

The person who loves kindly and not jealously will also, Paul insists, not be boastful. This means, surely, that he will not thrust himself forward, seeking admiration on the one hand or pity on the other. On the contrary, he will be ever ready to listen to others.

How clear, simple and translucent the love of which Paul speaks is! Yet how much effort it calls for every hour and every day of our lives if we are to overcome ourselves and achieve it! It is often the most insignificant and obvious things which help us to acquire the most profound attitude towards ourselves and others. But, in our attempt to make these obvious things (which we take so much for granted) realities in our daily lives, we often begin to perceive that they are not so obvious and that they cannot simply be accepted without question.

Love is not arrogant or rude. Love does not insist on its own way. Paul now approaches his task from another direction, using as it were the concave mirror of negation to reveal the shape of love. We should note the order in which he lists these negative attributes of love. The first is that love is not arrogant or, more literally, not inflated—'not puffed up' in the older translation. This points to a very important quality of love which is at once visible—especially in the image that Paul uses—but which can be expressed in words only with difficulty.

The man who truly loves does not make himself bigger than he really is. He does not fill himself with emptiness. He does not regard himself, his intentions or his aspirations as too important, does not give them an exaggerated value. He does not fill the entire sphere of human existence with himself—on the contrary, he prefers to withdraw to the periphery to allow life to move freely and to thrive. He does not fill himself with meaningless, unimportant things, but leaves room for the other person's life to flow into his own, opens himself to the other's vitality, happiness, ideas and feelings. The loving man fills himself from the other person. It is indeed only the man who can receive the gift of his neighbour's being who really loves. Being 'puffed up' is denying all room to the other person and placing exclusive emphasis on oneself. Love, on the other hand, means restraint, inner detachment, never stressing oneself. Love under-emphasizes itself, takes little account of itself, gives to others what it probably denies itself and is even glad that others are greater. Such love is a pure love.

This pure quality of love can be seen in that love is 'not rude'. Paul is not moralizing here—he is pointing rather to an inner process, the sensitivity of the person who loves. It is not possible to love rudely or oafishly because one is so completely seized by the other person's whole being that one has to be polite towards him. This cour-teous attitude arises, as it were, from an inner impulse. Its opposite, the brutalization of love, is expressed in the disappearance of polite behaviour. There is an element of nobleness in love—it acknowledges the other person's essential goodness and makes him feel that he is valued. It tones down our natural violence and ensures that noth-ing disastrous or painful will occur in our relationships. This polite aspect of love means, above all, that life is made possible for other people, that unpleasant situ-ations will be smoothed over, that other people's vulner-ability will be borne in mind and that their dignity will be respected.

This results in the essential definition of love, that it does not insist on its own way. This is, however, infinitely difficult. At some time or another, each one of us experi-ences a certain disgust—it is so humiliating to be the person we are, always the same, always leading the same miserable existence. We all want to get on in the world, even at somebody else's expense. We believe that we are disappointed by everyone and can escape from ourselves. There is in this a danger which threatens the very essence of love, namely the temptation to use other people to give strength and support to ourselves. How can we overcome the urge to do this?

Once again, we are brought to the ultimate limit of what can be expressed in words. The only possible answer to this question is, I think, that we can overcome this impulse only by loving. The great mystery of love is that it is a detachment from oneself which defies further investigation and which can 'playfully overcome', as Karl Barth observed, the dark temptation which 'tries to overcome love in people who love'. By loving, love cannot simply seek itself—it is incapable of doing this.

Paul's thought now takes a fresh turning once more and he describes the victory of love in everyday life.

Love is not irritable or resentful; it does not rejoice at wrong, but rejoices in the right.

An essential aspect of love is that in it we are released from a negative attitude. Our fellow men do not get on our nerves, annoy us or drive us into an attitude of hostility towards them. On the contrary, love completely overcomes all irritability and animosity. It does this, above all, by not being resentful; in other words, by not listing the other person's failings or, to translate Paul's text more literally, by not making an account of his evil. The man who loves authentically is simply unable to pronounce that completely perverse saying, unfortunately so often heard: 'I can forgive, but I cannot forget'. Reckoning, making an account of evil, can in time result in the person whom we love most of all becoming a monster, something that we can no longer bear to see or be with. So one of the most essential qualities of love is that it does not reckon or make entries in the accounts.

The 'released' attitude of love, moreover, has nothing to do with the mentality that 'rejoices at wrong' or with the meanness of spirit that derives satisfaction from another person's mistakes or from the thought that he has at last made a complete fool of himself. Love is absent from the life of a person who rejoices at wrong in this way. It is only a step from this to pride, to daring to say to the God who was crucified and rejected for us: 'Lord, I thank thee that I am not like other men, extortioners, unjust, adulterers, or even like this tax collector' (Luke 18.11). The man who loves, on the other hand, is, according to Paul, a man who 'rejoices in the right'. This love is a deep joy in the element of light in the other person's existence. A profound benevolence. I rejoice that the other person has reached a higher level of consciousness, or freedom, perhaps even of success, of selflessness and of self-surrender. This is the attitude with which God has confronted us since the creation of the world and will continue to confront us in eternity and which John defined in very simple words, but words which express the very essence of Christian faith: 'God is greater than our hearts' (1 John 3.20). To be able to rejoice sincerely in the other person's fine and admirable characteristics is one of the greatest of all acts of selfless love.

Mature love

The demands that have been made in the verses that we have considered so far are so overwhelming that Paul seems at this point to become suddenly aware of the fact that the level of love in the form in which he has outlined it simply cannot be reached by man. We have therefore to be patient with ourselves. If we really want to learn how to love, we must again and again make a new beginning, at the same time persisting in what we can still continue to do despite repeated failures. We must, in other words, allow our love gradually to become mature. Paul suggests four points of departure in this process of growth.

Love bears all things, believes all things, hopes all things, endures all things. He first introduces four simple concepts—bearing, believing, hoping and enduring. How often we are exploited when we love! We are so vulnerable in love, losing ourselves and being treated as playthings. How often the other person seems to make light of our love. The disappointment that results when the other does not respond to our love has to be borne, endured in faith and hope. How often we feel tired of loving and long to give it up. We find it impossible to bear the failure of trying to go on loving, we cannot believe the other person any more because we feel that we are being deceived—and may even have proof of it. We can no longer hope for any radical change. Such a love cannot, we think, possibly endure.

If we are honest, however, we must try to look at the matter from the other side. There are clearly situations in which what we believed was love has never become a real state of togetherness, and in such cases we should go no further. On the other hand, if we have already entered into what may be a painful relationship, we should then bear, believe, hope and endure. What would become of our world if no one were to persist in loving?

These four qualities of mature love fundamentally express one single attitude—that I make it possible, by my selfless love, for the other person to love as well, for him to feel, when I am with him, that he is quite secure with me, that he can be himself, the person he is or would like to be, that I do not restrict him, do not reproach him for being what he is, do not see him simply as he ought to be. It may be that new possibilities will be brought to life within him, not at once, of course, but gradually, as love continues to flow into him. I may succeed in this way in awakening him to his real humanity.

Love never ends; as for prophecies, they will pass away; as for tongues, they will cease; as for knowledge, it will pass away. Here Paul returns to his first idea, but does so, as it were, by way of a spiral staircase ascending to a higher level. At the end of our life, we shall not possess our achievements or our gifts—our real and eternal life is built up simply and solely of this bearing the burden of love. Everything that we have ever known, everything that has so profoundly shaken us throughout our life, everything that we have been able to express in language, everything that we have ever done to control the world, all our achievements—all this will pass away in a radical transformation. Only love is radically unchangeable. Only love will accompany us intact when we enter the area of eternal fulfilment. Love is the presence of the promise already fulfilled. This thought is expressed in Paul's statement about perfection and imperfection, in which our successes are given a relative value:

For our knowledge is imperfect and our prophecy is imperfect; but when the perfect comes, the imperfect will pass away. We can never really complete or fulfil anything in life. Our desires, longings and aims reach out into the future, but their realization always lags behind. Only love lasts. Everything else can only be carried out

53

imperfectly, in part. What may have seemed to us years or even only months ago to be quite obvious, something that we took completely for granted, is suddenly seen to be wretched and meaningless, perhaps not entirely value-less, but certainly imperfect.

When this happens, we become aware of a deeper level of experience, of a longing for quiet recollection, of a need to pause and reflect. We have, however, to learn what to do during this silence; otherwise, something will wither away in us and we shall remain at the mercy of frag-mentary thoughts, and restless desires and fears. We have to learn how to dwell on one really serious question or one really important thought. It is only when we have made this practice of silence a way of life that we shall begin to have a true inward experience and that some-thing will emerge from our existence—wisdom, quiet understanding or simply love.

Love remains. Only love can make life truly one, re-concile differences, overcome divisions, achieve a har-mony between the contrasts and contradictions that make our thinking and speaking so difficult or make us at one with our friends, with nature and with ourselves. With-out love, we ourselves remain imperfect, strangers in a strange world. This is why Paul goes on to say: *When I was a child, I spoke like a child, I thought like a child, I reasoned like a child; when I became a man, I gave up childish ways.*

Paul is not speaking against the childlike quality that is praised so highly in the gospels: that simplicity and directness of heart so characteristic of children. He is not opposed to that inherent ability to perceive and to be fully conscious without any ulterior intention that

54

children possess. All of these are distinctively human qualities which are both noble and very difficult for an adult to acquire. Paul is referring here to the childish characteristic in man which prevents him from becoming mature and which makes him cling to what is passing. We say that a child is *childlike*, but that an adult who goes through life as if it were a game, without accepting his responsibilities, is *childish*. This irresponsible and childish way of thinking, speaking, acting and judging prevents a man from loving.

Love, after all, brings with it a special kind of seriousness, even a threatening need. In love, we have to persist. We cannot play with love or act irresponsibly with it. It is by exposing ourselves to the care, the gravity and the fatigue of love that we grow towards what is essential in life and becomes mature. It is only in that way and in the degree to which we grow towards love that 'birth' will take place in our lives. But towards what future is this human birth which takes place in love directed?

The future of love
What precisely is the promise of life that has become mature in love? Paul expresses this promise in three sentences.

The first is *For now we see in a mirror dimly, but then face to face.* Our seeing now, Paul says, is fragmentary. partial, always reversed, as in a mirror, and always, because the mirror that he had in mind was of polished metal, very indistinct, a reflection with vague outlines. Our experience of the ultimate reality of God is in concepts and notions. It is not an experience of direct personal encounter with him. Our experience of almost everything is reversed—God is very close to us, yet we think of him as far away; he is far from us, but we think that he is near.

Then, however (that is, when we really love), Paul continues, this way of seeing and experiencing will be totally transformed. God will become a person whom we shall see 'face to face'. We shall see each other directly, without any intermediary. We shall be personally in touch with each other. According to the degree to which I love, something will happen between God and me, the experience which friends and lovers glimpse fleetingly in moments of supreme awareness—that I am you and you are me. Love can, Paul suggests, be fulfilled absolutely.

Now I know in part, then I shall understand fully, even as I have been understood. This apparently insignificant second sentence contains the whole promise of our life on earth. We shall know God as he knows us. In other words, we shall enter his immediate presence and see him directly. We shall still be creatures, but we shall understand God with every fibre of our being as he understands us. Basically, this means that we shall become God. The fundamental dynamism of my existence on earth is a movement, a growth into the absolute.

So faith, hope and love abide, these three; but the greatest of these is love. Even in this eternal confrontation, faith and hope remain in a very real sense, even though they will be transformed into a direct relationship with God. Faith remains as a constant state of being face to face with each other and a loving desire to receive. Hope remains as an ability and a will to receive even more of the eternal love. But these two must change their earthly forms. They will not exist then in the obscure and ever shifting forms that they have here on earth—they will remain as a bright, radiant and happy growing into a similarly ever-growing God.

In the second century AD, Irenaeus of Lyons commented on this passage in Paul: 'God must always be the greater, not only in this world, but also in eternity. He is always the one who teaches and man is always the one who learns. As the Apostle has said, when everything else has passed away, these three will remain—faith, hope and love. Our faith in God our teacher remains unshakable and we hope to receive even more from him . . . because he is goodness and because he possesses inexhaustible wealth and a kingdom without end.'

But why is love the greatest of these? It is because only love can be fulfilled without changing its present form. Our faith and hope are at present fragmentary. They remain in eternity, but have to be given an essentially new form, that of a certain, peaceful movement or growth into God which is also eternal because God is infinite. Only love, however, remains then as it is now—if and in so far as it is really love. This means that love can and must, even now, be interpreted as the ultimate anticipation of the ultimate. It is the presence of heaven in our life here on earth, the presence of the ultimate in our imperfect existence here and now. Love is also the mystery of Jesus's birth.

Promise

Promise

We cannot do better, when meditating on the mystery of Jesus's birth, than to think about another mystery—that of a young woman who called herself 'Sister Teresa of the Child Jesus'. Perhaps she can tell us more than the earnest and important men of whom we hear so much.

Teresa of Lisieux was only twenty-four when she died. A great deal has been written about her and many people have prayed to her and thought about her 'Little Way' of holiness. Although there is much piety in her writings, there is also much that is contradictory. Her language was florid, but her style, like her way of life, was also often bold and daring. She lived with reckless abandon.

What has Saint Teresa to say to us that is relative to our meditation? If we are to understand the mission of this quite extraordinary girl, we must look into her autobiographical writings. These are now available in their original form.[1] Like most unusual people, Teresa thought

[1] Thérèse of Lisieux, *Autobiography of a Saint*, The complete and authorised text of *L'Histoire d'une âme*, translated by Ronald Knox, with a Foreword by Vernon Johnson (London, 1958: the page numbers of quotations and citations in this meditation refer to this edition); *Therese vom Kinde Jesus. Selbstbiographische Schriften* (Einsiedeln, 1958); André Combes, *Sainte Thérèse de Lisieux et sa mission* (Paris, 1955); *Thérèse von Lisieux, Geschichte einer Seele und weitere Selbstzeugnisse*, collected, translated and introduced by Otto Karrer (Lugano, 1947).

in images. This is an extremely subtle way of combining the tension within the soul with the earthly element, and of expressing the mysteries inherent in the writer's concrete existence. If we wish to understand the mystery of Teresa's life, we must first look carefully at the images in which she saw her life's task reflected. What, then, were the images that figured most prominently in her spiritual life? The first that comes to mind is clearly connected with the mood of Christmas.

The stars: 'Sunday passed too quickly . . . not without a hint of melancholy. Up to the time of Compline, I remember, my happiness was unalloyed; it was during Compline that I said to myself: "The day of rest will soon be coming to an end." Tomorrow I should have to pick up life again, do my work and learn my lessons—it gave me the sense of being an exile, longing for the eternal rest of heaven, those endless sabbaths . . . On the way home I would look up at the stars that shone so quietly and the sight took me out of myself. In particular there was a string of golden beads (Orion's belt) which seemed, to my great delight, to be in the form of the letter T. I used to show it to Papa and tell him that my name was written in heaven' (pp. 66–7). We should not forget, when we read this, that Teresa's 'memories' were not simply memories, but interpretations of God's presence in her life.

The child: Teresa always thought of herself as a child. In answer to the question: 'What would you do if you could begin your religious life all over again from the beginning?', she replied: 'I think I would do the same again . . . I could never fear damnation. Little children are not damned. They are judged with special leniency.

It is possible too to remain a child even in the most res-
ponsible tasks. Is it not said of them that the Lord will be
exalted in order to comfort all the gentle and lowly on
earth?'

She also maintained that perfection had always seemed
to her to be something quite simple. 'It is sufficient to recognize that one is nothing and to place oneself like a
child in the arms of God. All the fine books that I cannot understand, let alone put into practice, I leave to
greater souls and exalted spirits. I am glad that I am little,
because the heavenly banquet is reserved for children and
for those who are like them.'

'For some time past', Teresa wrote, 'I have indulged
the fancy of offering myself up to the Child Jesus as a
plaything, for him to do what he liked with me. I don't
mean an expensive plaything; give a child an expensive
toy, and he will sit looking at it without daring to touch
it.

'But a toy of no value—a ball, say—is all at his disposal: he can throw it on the ground, kick it about, make
a hole in it, leave it lying in a corner, or press it to his
heart if he feels that way about it. In the same way, I
wanted Jesus to do exactly what he liked with me . . .
and he'd taken me at my word' (p. 171).

All this shows us how mature this attitude of being
a child in God's presence is. There is nothing sentimental
about it. Above all, we are aware of the positive value of
Teresa's conviction that we should place ourselves entirely at the mercy of the whims of a child and that, because that child is God-man, we shall, by doing this, come
closer to God.

The sea: 'I was seven or eight years old when Papa took

63

us to Trouville, and I shall never forget the impression made on me by my first sight of the sea. I couldn't take my eyes off it, its vastness, the ceaseless roaring of the waves, spoke to me of the greatness and the power of God . . . That evening, about the time when the sun looks as if it were sinking into an endless waste of waves, and leaving a long track of light in between, Pauline and I were sitting on a rock by ourselves watching it . . . For a long time I sat there thinking about this track of light and of its heavenly counterpart—the grace which pierces the darkness and guides the little white-sailed ship on its course. Sitting there beside Pauline, I made a resolve that I would always think of our Lord as watching me' (pp. 74–5).

This is another indication of how directly God flowed into the soul of this child through his creation. She consciously chose to find God in all things.

The Little Flower: 'If a wild flower could talk, I imagine it would tell us quite candidly about all God has done for it; there would be no point in hushing up his gifts to it, out of mock humility, and pretending that it was ugly . . . Anyhow, this isn't going to be the autobiography of a flower like that. On the contrary, I'm delighted to be able to put them on record, the favours our Lord has shown me, all quite undeserved' (p. 36).

Let us try to understand this 'florid' but honest language. Teresa thought of herself as a flower, a little wild flower. She grew out of the earth and flowered without any merit on her part or any effort. She was simply a gift of grace.

The basket: 'A day came when Léonie, thinking she was

too old now to play with dolls, came along to us with a
basket full of dresses and pretty little bits of stuff for
making others, with her own doll lying on the top. "Here
you are, darlings," she said, "choose which of these you'd
like; they're all for you." Céline put her hand in and
brought out a little ball of silken braid which had taken
her fancy. I thought for a moment, and then said, as I held
out my hand: "I choose the whole lot!" Then, without
further ceremony, I took over the whole basket . . . Only
a childish trait, perhaps, but in a sense it's been the key to
my whole life' (p. 51).

Later, Teresa wrote: 'Forgive me, Jesus, if I overstep
the bounds of right reason in telling you about these
longings and hopes of mine, which overstep all bounds;
and heal the hurt of my soul by granting all these wishes
fulfilment. To be betrothed to you, to be a Carmelite . . .
surely that ought to be enough for anybody? But, somehow, not for me . . . I feel as if I were called to be a
fighter, a priest, an apostle, a doctor, a martyr; as if I
could never satisfy the needs of my nature without per-
forming, for your sake, every kind of heroic action at
once.

'I feel as if I'd got the courage to be a Crusader . . .
dying on the battle-field in defence of the Church. And
at the same time, I want to be a priest; how lovingly I'd
carry you in my hands when you came down from heaven
at my call . . . Insignificant as I am, I long to enlighten
men's minds as the prophets and doctors did; I feel the call
of an Apostle. I should like to travel all over the world,
making your name known and planting your cross on
heathen soil; only I shouldn't be content with one
particular mission, I should want to be preaching the

gospel on all five continents and in the most distant islands, all at once. And even then it wouldn't do, carrying on my mission for a limited number of years; I should want to have been a missionary ever since the creation, and go on being a missionary till the world came to an end . . . What are you going to say to all these fond imaginations of mine? . . . Why, in consideration of my weakness, you found a way to fulfil my childhood's ambitions, and you've found a way now to fulfil these other ambitions of mine, world-wide in their compass' (pp. 233-4).

How wonderfully consistent Teresa's spiritual life was. Both as a little girl and later as a nun, she wanted to have everything—first the basket and then absolutely everything. And in the end she received everything.

Nature: 'Our eyes were lost in distance, as we watched the pale moon rising slowly above the height of the trees. Those silvery rays she cast on a sleeping world, the stars shining brightly in the blue vault above us, the fleecy clouds floating by in the evening wind—how everything conspired to turn our thoughts towards heaven! How beautiful it must be if this, the obverse side of it, was so calm and clear!' (p. 134). In another part of her autobiography, Teresa says: 'At all the critical moments of my life, I've found that nature seems to be the mirror of my own soul's condition: heaven shed tears in sympathy with me, and a cloudless sun shone brightly on my days of happiness' (p. 142).

Teresa's description of her experience in Switzerland, when she was on her way to Rome with the intention of asking Pope Leo XIII for his permission to enter the convent at the age of fifteen, is very interesting.

Switzerland: 'Rome was our goal, but there were plenty of wonderful experiences on the way there. Switzerland, where the mountain tops are lost in cloud, with its graceful pattern of waterfalls, its deep valleys where the ferns grow so high and the heather shows so red! How deeply it affected me, this lavish display of natural beauty! That God should have seen fit to squander such masterpieces on a world of exile . . . ! I was all eyes as I stood there, breathless at the carriage door; I wished I could have been on both sides of the compartment at once, so different was the scenery when you turned to look in the other direction. Now we were on the mountain side, with a bottomless chasm beneath ready to engulf us; now we would pass some delightful village, its chalets and its church tower covered with a soft canopy of snow-white cloud, or a wide lake at evening, with its calm surface reflecting at once the blue sky and the glow of sunset, till it has all the beauty of fairyland. Far away on the horizon we could see the great mountains, shadowy in outline except where their snow-clad tops showed dazzling in the sun, to complete the splendour of the view. The sight of these beauties made a deep impression on my thoughts. I felt as if I were already beginning to understand the greatness of God and the wonders of heaven' (pp. 157–8).

Do I have to add anything to this? Nothing, except gratitude that God has given us a country which, in 1887, inspired the soul of this holy young woman with such thoughts.

Wax and the canary: 'A relation of our nurse died quite young, leaving a family of three babies; and during her illness we took in the two little girls . . . Seeing these innocent souls at close quarters, I realized what a mistake

67

it is not to train them from the very start, when they are like wax to receive impressions . . . I saw what Jesus meant about hurting the conscience of "one of these little ones" ' (p. 146). This thought is at once taken to a deeper level in Teresa's description of another experience a little later —that of her pet birds.

'I had a canary once that sang to perfection; and at the same time I had a linnet which I tended with great care because I'd taken charge of it before it could fly. Born to captivity, it had no parents to learn from; but when it heard the canary trilling all day, it tried to follow suit. Not easy for a linnet; his gentle voice wasn't up to the shrill notes of his music master. It was touching to witness his efforts, but they succeeded in the end; without losing the sweetness of his voice, he sang in canary fashion' (p. 147).

Two impressive images of the spiritual life—the wax taught Teresa that man is fashioned by God and receives, as it were, his fingerprints and the linnet showed her that he can learn quite different 'tunes' from those that are inborn.

Penance: Before she entered the convent at Lisieux, Teresa prepared herself carefully, but perhaps rather strangely, for the great day.

'How did I pass those three months, a time, as it proved, so full of graces? My first thought was that perhaps I'd better give up living by a rather strict rule, as my habit had been of late . . . But before long I came to realize that this respite was a precious opportunity, and decided to give myself up, more than ever, to a recollected and mortified way of life. When I say 'mortified', I don't mean to suggest that I went in for penitential practices of any kind. That's a thing, I'm afraid, I've never done; I've heard so much about saintly people who took on the most rigorous mortifications from their childhood upwards, but I've never tried to imitate them—the idea never had any attractions for me . . . What I did try to do by way of mortification was to thwart my self-will; . . . to repress the rejoinder which sometimes came to my lips; to do little acts of kindness; . . . to sit upright instead of leaning back in my chair . . . That wasn't much, was it? But I did make these insignificant efforts to make myself less unworthy of a heavenly Bridegroom; and this period of apprenticeship has left tender memories behind it. Three months are soon past' (p. 181).

The most striking aspect of this account of Teresa's preparation for entering Carmel is the depth of her penetration into the mind of Christ. She clearly regarded the external practices of penance as of purely secondary importance. Her aim was above all to learn self-control and to prepare herself inwardly.

Snow: 'I forget if I've already mentioned what an attraction snow always had for me; even when I was quite tiny I loved to see the whiteness of it, and took delight in going for a walk when the flakes were falling on me. I wonder what was the reason for it? Perhaps because I was a winter flower myself, and nature was all dressed in white when I first looked out through the eyes of childhood. Anyhow, I'd always hoped that when I dressed in white to take the habit it would be in a white world; and now here was the eve of the great day, and nothing to be seen but a grey sky and a drizzle of rain' (pp. 190–1).

Another beautiful day spoilt—but is it so very important to have snow when one takes the habit?

Jesus's plaything: One day, Teresa writes, 'It was borne in upon me during my prayer that this eagerness to make my profession was mixed up with a good deal of self-love. After all, I'd given myself over to our Lord for his pleasure, his satisfaction, not mine, and here was I trying to see if I could get him to do my will, not his. Another thing occurred to me too; a bride's got to have a trousseau against her wedding day . . . So I told our Lord: . . . I'm ready to wait just as long as you want me to . . . In the meantime, I'll work hard at trying to make myself a lovely wedding dress . . . and when you see that it's ready, I know quite well that nothing in heaven or earth will prevent you from coming to me, and making me, once and for ever, your bride' (pp. 194–5).

This is yet another example of Teresa's profoundly serious intention shining through her childlike way of expressing herself. She reiterates here, in a different form, what she has already said, that she wants to be Jesus's little plaything—giving herself over to him *comme son petit jouet*—for him to do what he likes with her.

The canvas: 'If the canvas on which an artist is working could think and speak, it obviously wouldn't be annoyed with the brush that kept on touching and retouching it; and it wouldn't be envious either, because it would know perfectly well that all its beauty came from the artist who held the brush, not from the brush itself. And on the other side, the brush couldn't claim any credit for the masterpiece on which it was at work, because it would know quite well that artists are never at a loss; they are the sort of people who enjoy coming up against difficulties, and find it amusing, sometimes, to make use of shoddy and imperfect instruments.

'Well, I'm the poor little brush Jesus has picked out to be the means of imprinting his image on the souls which you have entrusted to me. An artist isn't content to work with one brush, he'll need at least two; there's the really valuable one which he sketches in the general colour scheme, covering the whole canvas in no time, and then there's the tiny one which fills in the details . . . I'm the little tiny brush which Jesus uses afterwards, to put in the extra flourishes' (p. 280).

Teresa tried in this way to put her mind at rest when she noticed that God was accomplishing great things in others' souls through her. There was, of course, no reason for her to do this, because no one really believed that she was able to do anything extraordinary.

Flight: 'In the last resort . . . my recipe for victory is to run away; I used to try this even in my novitiate, and I always found it worked . . . I have a strong feeling that it's better best not to engage in a battle when defeat is quite certain . . . When I look back at my novitiate, . . . it makes me laugh now, to think what heavy weather I made over nothing at all . . . At least I've learnt not to be surprised at anything—it doesn't worry me to discover that I am frailty itself; on the contrary, I go about boasting of it. Every day, I expect to find out a fresh lot of imperfections in my character' (pp. 269–70).

Surely this is a totally honest attitude towards Jesus which nothing can disguise or obscure. To conclude our meditation on the spirituality of Teresa, however, we must turn to the great image which she made well known and which made her well known—the image of the lift.

The lift: 'As you know, dear Mother, I've always wished that I could be a saint. But whenever I compared myself to the saints there was always a difference . . . However, I wasn't going to be discouraged; I said to myself: "God wouldn't inspire us with ambitions that can't be realised. Obviously there's nothing great to be made of me, so it must be possible for me to aspire to sanctity in spite of my insignificance. I've got to take myself just as I am, with all my imperfections; but somehow I shall have to find out a little way, all of my own, which will be a direct short-cut to heaven. After all (I said to myself) we live in an age of inventions. Nowadays, people don't even bother to climb the stairs—rich people, anyhow; they find a lift more convenient. Can't I find a lift which will take me up to Jesus, since I'm not big enough to climb the steep stairway of perfection?" So I looked in the Bible for some hint about the lift I wanted, and I came across the passage where Eternal Wisdom says: "Is anyone as simple as a child? Then let him come to me." To that Wisdom I went; it seemed as if I was on the right track; what did God undertake to do for the childlike soul that responded to his invitation? I read on, and this is what I found: "I will console you like a mother caressing her son; you shall be like children carried at the breast, fondled on a mother's lap" ' (pp. 248–9).

I do not think that this passage, the last of my quotations from Teresa of Lisieux, needs any comment.

What can I say in conclusion about this simple woman who died so young? All her life, she lived full of love for God made man, the child Jesus. She knew that this God was love and she sacrificed herself to that love, not as a sacrifice of righteousness, but simply to bear witness. Combes has observed that, as a witness to God's love, she constantly repeated the message: 'Do not be mistaken—

our God is not severe. He has no intention. He will not
repay evil with evil. Our God is infinite love and overcomes all weakness.' This is, of course, the message of
Jesus's birth. It is also a promise.

God's birth in us

God's birth in us

I would like to consider a very simple idea to which John
Tauler drew attention as long ago as the fourteenth century—the threefold birth of Christ. In reflecting about
these three aspects of Christ's birth, we shall be extend-
ing our meditation to its cosmic dimensions. Tauler
thought of the three traditional masses of Christmas day
as representing three elements—Christ's birth in the
Trinity, his birth in history and his birth in us. Let us think
about each of these elements in turn.

Christ's birth in the Trinity
This birth is celebrated at midnight and the mass begins
with the words: 'The Lord said to me: "You are my son,
today I have begotten you"' (Ps. 2.7). This first mass
points to the hidden birth of the Son of God which took
place in the Trinity. If we really want to fathom the profound mystery of the birth of Jesus, we must first consider this mystery of mysteries, the eternal process of the
Trinity. God, revelation tells us, is three in one. He is a
process in which he personally confronts himself and so
loves the one who is opposite him, his Son, that his love
is a person, the Holy Spirit. God is therefore eternally
coming into being, eternally as the witness, the Father,
eternally proceeding, as the Son, and eternally as circling

love, the Holy Spirit. As creatures, we are intimately connected with this process of the Trinity. By bearing the
features of the second person of the Trinity, by living,
feeling and thinking, we who are created fulfil the life of
God himself in a mysterious way in the world. Our re-
semblance to Jesus is such that we men, really living and
the recipients of grace, are the temples of the Holy
Spirit. Living the Christian life and praying as Christians
in the world, our aim is to experience that world as the
vehicle and dwelling-place of God.

Christ's birth in history

The second mass opens with the words: 'Today a light
will shine upon us' (Isa. 9.2). The Son of God became
man one night two thousand years ago in a little village
called Bethlehem. He was laid in a manger and wrapped
in swaddling clothes. His mother nursed him. He was
like all babies, a tiny helpless thing. He shared our human
fate entirely. He grew up, almost unnoticed and mis-
understood. He encountered hostility everywhere and led
a wretched life, surrounded by unimportant people, imprisoned, so to speak, inside a wall of misunderstanding.
Our God was very small—the very smallness and un-
importance of our God is a great mystery. Christ made
humility a fundamental law of the new creation. This is
the great mystery of Christmas which was made known
in Bethlehem two thousand years ago.

Christ's birth in us

The third mass begins in the day: 'For to us a child is
born; to us a son is given' (Isa. 9.6). This symbolizes
the birth that takes place every day in each one of us.

78

In her book, *The Envoy of Divine Love*, Gertrude the Great wrote: 'One day, I entered the courtyard, sat down by the fishpond and considered the sweetness of the place. The limpidity of the flowing water, the green of the trees, the flight of the birds and of the doves in particular and above all the peacefulness of the place filled me with delight. I began to wonder what could be added to this place to make its joy complete.

'I must have a friend, I thought, a devoted and familiar friend, to make my loneliness sweet. You, my God, drew my thoughts to you. Certainly it was you who inspired me with them. You showed me that my heart could be a dwelling-place for you. Like this flowing water, I must be thankful for what you have suggested to me and direct the flow of my thoughts back to you. Like these trees, flourishing in the green of good works, I must increase in strength and devote myself to good works. Like these doves flying, I must raise myself towards heaven . . . In this way, my heart will provide you with a dwelling that is sweeter than any sweetness.

'The whole day long, my mind was full of this idea. In the evening, before I went to bed, when I kneeled to pray, I thought suddenly of the words of Scripture: "If a man loves me, he will keep my word, and my Father will love him, and we will come to him and make our home with him". Then I felt in my heart that you had come.'

Being a Christian means growing together with Christ. In the words of the Father of the Church: 'God became man so that man might become God'. The essence of God's becoming man was his emptying of himself. Every Christian is bound at some time or other in his life to come to the point where he is called to be humble and empty himself. He must at that point make his decision, and the real Christian decides to surrender completely and to live for the rest of his life in a spirit of self-surrender.

We realize the attitude of Jesus in our lives by leaving ourselves behind us in selfless love and service of others. He gives us heaven because, in the form of our brother, he was hungry and we gave him food, he was thirsty and we gave him drink, he was a stranger and we welcomed him, he was naked and we clothed him, he was sick and we visited him, he was in prison and we came to him. (Matt. 25.35–6). It would seem as though God had forgotten himself in his description of heaven and the judgment, because he appears only in the face of our neighbour. In heaven, what began in the Trinity, continued at Bethlehem and has been realized throughout the history of Christian life will be fully revealed.

In this way, Jesus prepares for his second and last coming in glory. This last Christmas in the world will continue in eternity. It is known as heaven.

Becoming man

Becoming man

'For us men and for our salvation he came down from heaven.' This is the answer given by the creed to the old question of Christology: 'Why did God become man?' Two reasons are provided in this answer. The first is that he became man 'for us men', in other words, so that man can really be himself, that is, man. The second reason is that God became man 'for our salvation': in other words, so that he might redeem us from guilt. These are Jesus's two basic functions in the history of man's salvation. They are, however, not equal in value and this difference is expressed in the order in which these two reasons are stated in the creed.

God became man in the first place to complete, in Christ, our humanity. Even if sin had not come into the world, Jesus would still have become man, but since man did in fact incur guilt (in other words, since he placed a distance between himself and God), Jesus first 'had to' reconcile us with God and become our redeemer. This second and subsequent function does not, however, cancel the primary reason for his becoming man, the act that had been foreseen and planned from the very beginning. Although he saved us from sin, he is above all the one who enables us to become fully and really human. This fulfilment of our humanity took place finally on the cross.

Jesus raises our humanity—and therefore also the universe, which is concentrated in us—up to the level of completion. In this sense, he is the God who lifts up. The ultimate statement that can be made about God, a statement which represents an absolute limit to human thought, is 'God became man'. Anything that we can say, feel or do pales into insignificance beside this statement. Any attempt to fathom it reveals how fragile human thought is. It is a statement that is frequently repeated, but we ought to be extremely careful when we make it, as careful as God himself, whose preparation for the incarnation took so long and who allowed this statement, 'God became man', to rise up very slowly and gently from the whole of man's experience.

What would have become of us if God were not so patient, if he did not let everything come to maturity with such gentle and attentive restraint? God is very forbearing with man, with the whole of his existence including his thinking. He is eternal and is neither fearful nor in a hurry. He knows how vulnerable we are and so he does not force us, intimidate us or press us. He stands quietly at our door and knocks very gently.

In this meditation, we should approach the mystery of God's incarnation from a point of view which is based on our experience as men, which we can discuss easily and which does not confuse us. For our point of departure, we can take Paul's statement: 'All things are yours, and you are Christ's, and Christ is God's' (1 Cor. 3.22-3). If we consider this text very attentively, we may be able to come closer to the heart of the ultimate mystery: that in Christ the world is completed and brought to fulfilment.

All things are yours. The incarnation of the world
One of the most striking aspects of present-day thinking
is its emphasis on man's increasing awareness of his
intimate connexion with the world. He no longer regards
the world as a static factor or as a framework that is already given and unchanging. On the contrary, he sees it as
an evolving process, a continuing development, something that is still in the course of becoming. He is aware
of the continued formation, for example, of the Milky
Way, the solar system and the planets, of the production
of increasingly complicated forms of life and of a tentative movement forwards and upwards to a higher level
of existence and consciousness.

Man knows that he is closely linked to this world and
regards himself as the product of an evolution that has
lasted for many millions of years, but also as the summit
of this evolutionary effort in the world. The universe ('all
things') is, as it were, dwelling within him. The place
where man is most radically connected with the universe
is his body. In and through the human body the world
changes into the spiritual, so that the human body is
also the place of change, in which the matter of the world
is united with the spirit. The essential aspect of the
spirit, however, is that it is infinitely open to the infinite.
This radical transformation of the material into the
spiritual is known simply as 'man', who is spirit become
body or body become spirit. This means that man is the
centre of the universe, of 'all things'. All the material
forces of the world are concentrated in him and these
forces thrust forward in him into the spiritual sphere.
Man is the highest unit of evolution in the world, combining in perfect unity body and spirit.

According to Christian thought, which reached one of its highest points in the theology of Thomas Aquinas, man is a unified being. In man, spirit and matter are essentially one. Man is not composed of two separate 'things', spirit and matter—he is one single being. From these two closely united factors comes a third which is neither one nor the other, the soul. The human soul is the highest development of the body. The teaching of Thomas Aquinas about the unity of the body and the soul enables us to gain some insight into man's intimate connexion with the world which we mentioned at the beginning of this section. This relationship between the body and the soul makes it possible for the universe to enter fully into the openness of the spirit. The human body, the product of an evolutionary process that has taken millions of years in the world, is really spirit. It is not simply that man's body shelters or contains spirit—spirit is inherent in man's body and essentially one with it.

The evolution of the universe reveals a distinct preference for more unified and more complex forms. This tendency is even clearer in the higher stages of evolution and it is in man that the world finally achieves its distinctive character of spirit. In this sense, then, the evolutionary process is the birth of man. This incarnation of the world has taken place since the very beginning of the development of the cosmos.

This cosmic incarnation must be seen everywhere, in each one of its phases, not simply in the creation of the human soul, as real creation. This arises from the very concept of evolution itself. Evolution, after all, means that a more develops from a less, that the world surpasses itself in its being. This is something that is happening not simply here and there and at certain times, but at every moment of the entire process of development. It would be quite wrong to think that God intervened again and again in his creation, as though the world were a machine which God tunes up to higher and higher performance in the course of time. On the contrary, the world itself develops —God does not develop the world. He is outside the chain of cause and effect in the world and is not a link in the chain of second causes. He creates the world by giving it the forces to create itself, to raise its level of being even higher and to evolve towards the spirit. In this sense, then, the world itself can be said to produce the human spirit in a process which does not in any way throw doubt on the creation by God of each individual human soul. Body and soul, we are completely children of this earth and in this we are also completely children of God.

We may, however, go a stage further and say that, as children of this earth, we already have God's life in us. To say simply that God creates us out of nothing is to define negatively God's creative activity. God's creation of man from himself, however, according to no law other than his own and under no influence but his own, is the positive aspect of that work of creation. All creation lives, in other words, as the thought and image of God. In this way, all creation is mysteriously but intimately connected with the second person of the Trinity. The Logos is the perfect expression of the first person of the Trinity, the Father, an image confronting the Father who is the Father himself. It is in this perfect image of God that the possibility of a creation is based, in other words, the possibility of an infinite image or copy of God. Every human is this image in so far as he bears the likeness of the second person of the Trinity.

If we combine this idea with the one outlined previously, that of a continuous creative process seen as evolution, we see that the world proceeds from the second person of the Trinity with creative newness from second to second, that the Logos is present with his creative activity at every point in the evolutionary process, creating his own image in the world. We may say, in other words, that the Son gives the world the ability to get along on its own, to use its own forces to work its way upwards towards him, 'for in him all things were created' (Col. 1.16) and 'all things were created through him and for him' (Col. 1.7). The temporary but real aim of the cosmic process is man. After a long period of tentative seeking, the evolutionary process of creation finds its ultimate form. A breach was at last made in matter when the human spirit was produced in the world and this has caused the biological forces of change to become gradually less powerful. With every year, every month and every hour, the spirit is created more and more in the world, with the result that knowledge, love and freedom are constantly increasing with the passage of time.

But what does all this mean in terms of the Christian's spiritual life in his day-to-day existence? In the first place and above all, it means that he lives in a holy world. It means that he must include the whole world in his Christian life and prayer. It means that he must try to experience Christ in all truth and in all creation. He must have boundless respect for every creature, be attentive to the whole of life, have good intentions for everyone and everything in creation, even the humblest, and be open to all truth, wherever it comes from. This is the first and most important demand imposed on us by this view.

In the second place, however, it means that we must try to understand that our humanity is holy and that we have to behave correspondingly towards our fellow men. Yet, while thinking of other people, we should not forget that we too are holy and that we must accept ourselves with all our limitations and weariness and with the desires and promises that are constantly breaking through our limitations. We have also to accept that we are what we have become, because it is from our concrete existence here and now that we have set out in search of God. This is not something that can simply be taken for granted. Our fellow men are holy and we must also honour and respect their holiness, recognize their distinctiveness, never violate their freedom, defend them if they are insignificant, vulnerable or helpless. In short, we must be polite towards each other, bearing constantly in mind that politeness includes consideration and deep sympathy for the other person's life, his difference from ourselves, his circumstances and his difficulties.

Finally and in the third place, it means that we should never be satisfied with what has already been done, with the situation that we have already reached. We must allow the impulse which has driven the universe to higher and higher stages of being in the evolutionary process and has become finally concentrated in man to go on working powerfully within us. We must therefore not have too exalted a view of ourselves, of our own achievements and structures or even of our own idea of 'God'. Above all, we must think of God as greater and more all-embracing than all our own imaginings—we must not restrict him to concepts and formulas. We must not delude ourselves into thinking that we have him in our grasp. We should not be mean in our attitude to life—ours and those of others. We have to allow ourselves to be carried by love beyond anything that we or others might achieve.

These three demands of our Christian understanding of creation in the sense of the incarnation of the world point the way to a new dimension of the incarnation. Since the world has been, so to speak, 'made man' in us and has produced us body and soul, we have the task of becoming more human. The incarnation is, in other words, not yet complete. The evolution of the world merely produced the matter from which we, through our own efforts, have to fashion ourselves into full men. This is the second aspect of the incarnation.

You are Christ's. The incarnation of man
There are many different paths which man can follow in his quest for completion of fulfilment, so many that it would be impossible for me to discuss them even briefly here. What is important for us to bear in mind in this context, however, is that man does not exist in the world in an already finished state—he is, as it were, only a preliminary design of his real self. There is in him a mysterious tension between what he is now and what he ought to be, between what he has already accomplished and what still remains to be achieved. The man who really aims to *be* has to begin again and again anew. This beginning is a constantly effective element in the condition of being man.

What it means is that man must continuously resolve anew to exist as man. To do this, he must, so to speak, be

brave enough to be a man, that is, to see dangers and confront them without retreating and to make use of even the
most difficult situations in order to grow more and more
fully into manhood. He must allow what is really vital and
what holds out the greatest promise for his future to
emerge from his innermost being. The early Christians
called this exertion the 'practice of virtue', a phrase which
strikes us nowadays as rather antiquated and which makes
us feel a little uneasy. But it is, on the contrary, a description which is most meaningful, as anyone who has experienced the bitterness of looking back at his life and
realizing that it had not turned out at all as it should have
done will admit.

Is it true, however, to say that man can complete himself of his own accord, that he can, by his own effort,
fulfil all the possibilities that are present in embryo within him? Fortunately or unfortunately, this is not the case.
And this, of course, brings us to the heart of the matter,
namely that it is impossible for man to attain the real
essence of his being as man, for him to fulfil himself completely as man. Man's being, in other words, infinitely
transcends itself.

I should like to develop this idea by analysing briefly
three basic functions of human reality. The first of
these is human knowledge. Acting in the sphere of knowledge, the human spirit has the task of appropriating a
concrete reality without in any sense violating what is
known. We begin to explore the world by gaining knowledge of individual objects and by gradually understanding the relationship between man and other living
organisms. We also learn how to deal with these relationships through acquiring knowledge. Increasing know-

ledge also reveals to us the laws governing nature, human society as a whole and personal relationships generally. The acquisition of isolated fragments or areas of knowledge in this way is undeniably valuable, but we also have to try, despite repeated failure, to relate these separate areas of knowledge to each other and to combine them together in a logically worked out system. In attempting to do this, we inevitably begin to sense the existence of something much more all-embracing which cannot be approached simply by combining together all our individual bits of knowledge.

This experience is sometimes accompanied by an insight into what can only be called the ground of all being, the reality which has so far eluded us and which is clearly capable of transforming the world. Once we have experienced this insight into the ultimate reality, we understand that our thirst for knowledge has always been motivated by something much more than mere curiosity. We become aware that we have already been attracted by an absolute, by the fulness of being. Drawn on by this absolute, we have discovered the concrete and individual things of everyday life, but these have never been able to satisfy our longing. In our quest for separate fragments of knowledge, we have always at the same time wanted to know the God who is completely different. We are therefore always, at least implicitly, in search of God when we are seeking knowledge. In every limited sphere of knowledge, the absolute comes closer to us.

We may, then, conclude that our human knowledge will be completed when the absolute becomes a reality that can be fully grasped and unlimited being is completely contained within a limited being. Until that happens, then, man continues to long for the incarnation of God in every act of knowledge.

The second function is human longing. This is also divided between the unlimited nature of the demands that it makes and the limited extent to which it can be realized. Man is always dissatisfied with any success in the world. A mysterious element within him urges him constantly onwards towards new promises, new aims and new achievements. An inexorable necessity drives him on towards something more, but every attempt to fulfil his longing is condemned to failure.

This is why we often, perhaps too often, pause on the way and accept what is temporary as ultimate. This, however, usually results in unhappiness and a sense of unfulfilment, which we may not even admit to ourselves. If we are completely honest, then, we do not try to live without longing, but continue to strive towards the infinite even in our everyday lives.

Throughout history, man has always been drawn by the unknown, which has seemed to him to be more beautiful than what he already has or knows and therefore worth every effort to reach—and this is still so today. His genesis, in other words, is still in progress and every time he is fulfilled he must at once begin his search again. A taste for happiness, a basic optimism, a hope that he will find even greater fulfilment—these are fundamental to human life. The Apostle Paul was clearly aware that man was driven by his very nature to 'walk in newness of life' (Rom. 6.4), but he was also conscious of the burden imposed by this way of life: 'So we do not lose heart. Though our out-

ward nature is wasting away, our inner nature is being re-
newed every day' (2 Cor. 4.16).

This means that man has within him a dynamic tendency towards what is humanly within his grasp: in other
words, what is given to him as grace is at the same time
what he of necessity wants. It is only possible for his longing to be fulfilled when he is confronted with the object
of that longing, when the absolute is completely contained
within what can be reached and grasped, in other words,
when God becomes man. At the centre of all man's longings, then, is God.

This brings us to the third function of the reality of
man's existence—human love. Love exists when two per-
sons enter into a unity of being, when they say of that
being not 'I' but 'we'. It is a process in which two people
live entirely from each other. The ultimate intention of
love, however, goes far beyond anything that can be
achieved here and now by this love. Love anticipates, in
its present form, this ultimate fulfilment and completion.
What man is looking for in love is something un-
conditional, unlimited and infinite which lies beyond what
is conditional, limited and finite. Limited love is an im-
possibility. In our striving towards the infinite, then, we
make a fragile, finite being the object of our love. This is a
demand that no person can ever fully satisfy, because, however greatly that person is loved, he is not equal to the
love that flows towards him.

Love therefore has to struggle every day against the
force of the evidence that 'you are limited' and in a
desperate attempt to attribute an unlimited character to
this limitation. Anyone who has ever loved knows that
this is the real temptation of human love and that it is

this which gives us a certain insight into the meaning of Louis Aragon's poem, 'There is no happy love'. Human love simply cannot be fulfilled. The absolute therefore has to be present completely in a finite person, so that the real object of man's love is, in other words, God who has become man. Whenever man loves sincerely, his inner intention always includes the incarnate God.

I shall now try to summarize the first two elements, knowledge and longing, and to bring them together. The evolutionary process in the world is transformed in man, living in him in his restless hopes, dreams and desires as an orientation towards the infinite on the part of a finite creature. This concentration of the whole of evolution in the human reality produces in us an enormous pressure of ideas and desires. A process of fermentation is going on inside us all the time, a process in which the universe is struggling upwards in us towards the absolute.

We can therefore understand now how 'all things were created for him', how, in other words, all creation and all creative energy is directed towards Jesus Christ. The birth of the Son of God is therefore not an isolated event which took place without reference to the evolution of the universe. On the contrary, the incarnation is the completion of the universe and the fulfilment of man's existence. God as it were had to enter history because he created the world to move towards him. 'All things are yours, and you are Christ's.' We must now consider the third statement made in this text:

Christ is God's. The incarnation of God
Now that we have prepared the way for an understanding of the almost incomprehensible event of the incar-

nation by approaching it as far as possible from the van-
tage-point of our own experience, we can at last pronounce
that most mysterious of all sentences: God became man.
As we have seen, nothing is more reasonable than this
statement. Without it, the whole world and the whole
human reality would be unthinkable. But our task now is
to make a supreme effort and try to understand the
tremendous nature of what we have been discussing so
far. The best approach may be to analyse briefly the three
elements of this statement in turn: 'God', 'God becomes',
and 'God becomes man'.

Firstly, *God*. Man cannot grasp or understand this
name, which stands for something that is far beyond him.
Thinking about God, he is tempted simply to bring together everything that he knows in the world and above
all in himself, everything that is beautiful and exalted,
all his longings and the fulfilment of all his desires, in
other words, all that is best in him and regard this as
'God'. The temptation, then, is to worship himself and in
this way to destroy everything, since he can never fulfil
his longings, which must always be beyond his reach. God
can never be thought of as composed of anything that
is found in this world. Man can only be fulfilled by what
is completely different. He can only speak about this fulfilment if he denies, in the same breath, what has just
been said. It may be that our profound experience of God
nowadays as the completely different one is a sign of very
special grace. It is also possible that man has to endure
this terrible experience of God's being very far away so
that he may begin to feel how radically different God really
is.

Secondly, *God becomes*. If we believe that the most sublime and the most pure thoughts can be expressed about God, then we seem bound also to say that God cannot become. He is the one who infinitely is above all change and all passing away. He is the 'unmoved mover' who is self-sufficient and dependent on nobody. That is a very exalted and beautiful concept of God, but it is fundamentally wrong. It is true that we cannot think of God in any other way, yet he *is* different in fact. How is he different from the concept? How can he be known as the one who is not simply completely different and far from us?

It is, of course, in the light of his revelation of himself at Christmas that we experience him not only as completely different from ourselves, but as like us, not only as distant, but at the same time as near to us. Our God has appeared to us—'Philip, he who has seen me has seen the Father' (John 14.9). The God of revelation comes and goes. He prepares his coming with great care and after he has come to us he goes away from us, tearing himself, as it were, from us. He becomes a little child, lives inconspicuously among us, learns how to be a carpenter, travels around a good deal, becomes tired, even exhausted and completes his work afraid, sweating blood and crying out that God has forsaken him. The idea of a static and exalted God may be difficult for us to grasp, but that of a God who becomes is totally bewildering. Our bewilderment is increased as soon as we begin to consider the third element in the statement:

God becomes man. It is a strange fact that, although we long with all our being for God's presence, as soon as he comes to us, we can no longer endure it. There are many examples of this in the Bible—man's encounter with God in his revelation of himself is painful and brings about a revolution in his life. When God appears, man must hide his face. He falls as though dead. He conceals himself from God, as our earliest ancestors did in a profoundly symbolic gesture. 'Whither shall I flee from thy presence?' the psalmist cried, 'If I ascend to heaven, thou art there! If I make my bed in Sheol, thou art there!' (Ps. 139.7–8). A stranger looks unflinchingly at us and, like Job, we cry out: 'How long wilt thou not look away from me, nor let me alone till I swallow my spittle?' (Job 7.19). At Sinai, the frightened people of Israel beseeched Moses: 'You speak to us and we will hear, but let not God speak to us, lest we die' (Exod. 20.20).

In his incarnation, however, God breaks through this experience. He appears as a child, helpless in the crib and needing the love and care of his people, his creatures. He no longer threatens man, but appeals to him. Just before Jesus's appearance, John the Baptist spoke threateningly about what Christ would do when he came, but in fact he proved to be a man who was full of goodness and understanding who defended sinners and weak people not only from other people, but even from his Father. Christ stood up for us, so completely that Paul was able to say: 'If we are faithless, he remains faithful, for he cannot deny himself' (2 Tim. 2.13). From the time of Christ's coming, it has been impossible to think of anything that is human—apart from sin—which is not at the same time applicable to God. Christ transformed God's power into grace and goodness.

The God of the incarnation, then, is both infinitely far and infinitely near, both incomprehensibly different from us and yet very similar to us. All that is good and beautiful in the world is present in him and yet all this goes far beyond any possible fulfilment on earth and enters his life, the life of God. From now on, there is only one event in the world—the mysterious birth of Christ; and this is the real meaning of Christmas for us today, because the shepherds are no longer out in the field and the child Jesus is no longer in his crib in Bethlehem. That all happened in the past. One thing, however, remains today Christ's birth in humanity, the birth of the 'cosmic' Christ.

One of the most profound insights in the whole of Paul's teaching is that, although Christ really came in history, he is still coming and will continue to come until the end of the world. Christ's birth takes place throughout the whole of history and at the end of time there will be the fulness of Christ, the *plerōma*. Christians build up his body. That is their Christmas in the world. It is also the meaning of the sacraments and of the whole of the Christian way of life. In their lives, Christians—both those who profess their faith publicly and those whose Christianity is anonymous—enter into Christ and build him up. When the measure of Christ is full, when all those comprise the fulness of Christ's being have grown up into him, the 'cosmic' Christ will have been born, heaven will be present and the first creation will be complete. It is then that life will really begin and that the extraordinary adventure of the world will end.

What does all this mean for us in our lives here and now? It means that we should live in such a way that we go beyond our limitations and enter the sphere that is beyond our understanding. We must accept that our dissatisfaction is inspired by God and that we must again and again overcome the narrowness of our existence. God has created us for himself and we are bound to be restless until we have found him, the infinite one.

Nothing is great enough for man, weak though he is. To be human is a breath-taking experience. God is constantly drawing us onwards out of our habits and our narrow, small life. If we remain satisfied with what we have already achieved, we are clearly not being as God intended us to be. How, then, can we be completely open to the absolute? Simply by being each other's brothers and loving and serving our fellow men in our everyday lives. 'As you did it to one of the least of these my brethren, you did it to me' (Matt. 25.40). This is the greatest and most profound aspect of the mystery of Jesus's birth.

Incalculable God

Incalculable God

At the time of Jesus's birth, we again become aware of
the fact that God is different, that he has no habits, that
his ways are always new, that he is young and that, when
he comes to us, it is in the way that he chooses. Christmas
is therefore the feast of the incalculable God. But it is not
only then that he is incalculable. Even later, after his resurrection, he appeared quite surprisingly as a gardener,
as a hungry traveller and as a man on the shore of the lake:
on each occasion as someone who could be mistaken for
somebody else.

God comes unexpectedly and when he comes he is always different. His ways can never be calculated in advance. This can be a threat to the man who is looking for
him. How bold and uninhibited must have been the faith
of the men who first kneeled in the straw and worshipped
God in the child they found at Bethlehem. This thought,
that God is incalculable, gives us a suitable point of departure for a meditation on a theme that is hardly ever
considered seriously or, if it is considered at all, is only
mentioned incidentally—the theme of the temptations of
Christmas.

The first temptation is that God cannot be tied down.
Because he is so incalculable, man can never have him in
his power. He can never hold God or do what he wants

with him. He always eludes man's grasp. He cannot be bound by rules, systems or methods. Even the saints fell into this trap sometimes; they tried again and again to coerce God with a great number of prayers, numerous provisos, and long hours of contemplation. They longed to have him, his word and his revelation wholly at their disposal all the time, and to experience his grace and his consolation constantly. But God taught them a better way.

It was right for man to prepare the way for God, to lift up every valley and to make low every mountain and hill, by prayer, by conquering his self-will and above all simply by living well every day of his life. But it was entirely up to God whether he chose to walk along the way prepared for him, or whether he preferred a different way; whether he wanted to enter by the door that had been decorated so festively for him, or whether he went in by another door altogether. We are therefore bound to conclude that the only real attitude that the saint can have is simply to be ready and available, to persist, to open his soul to God and to spread out his arms to receive him. God will be present for him when and where and in whatever way God pleases.

Paul expresses this question of man's relationship with God in incomprehensible terms in his Letter to the Romans: 'I will have mercy on whom I have mercy, and I will have compassion on whom I have compassion. So it depends not upon man's will or exertion, but upon God's mercy' (Rom. 9.15–16). The same attitude emerges in a most impressive way from Psalm 127: 'Unless the Lord builds the house, those who build it labour in vain. Unless the Lord watches over the city, the watchman stays awake in vain. It is in vain that you rise up early and go late to rest, eating the bread of anxious toil; for he gives to his beloved sleep'.

The best way to prepare for God's coming unexpectedly into our lives is by silence. This is why, in the Christmas liturgy, we sing: 'While all things were in quiet silence, and that night was in the midst of its swift course, thy almighty word leapt down from heaven out of the royal throne' (Wis. 18.14–15). The Apostolic Father, Ignatius, Bishop of Antioch, called Christ, in his letter to the Magnesians, 'the Word proceeded from silence'. Even those who were not believers had some inkling of this connexion between God's presence and silence. Heraclitus, for example, maintained that the authentic attitude of the spirit was one of 'listening quietly to the truth of things', a silence before the mystery. It is in silence that we experience the constant newness of God. We prepare ourselves best for his incalculable ways when we are silent.

The second temptation of Christmas is that God often disappoints us. How is this little child to keep his hands firmly on the reins and curb the world? It would seem, however, that God is weak and helpless in all his government of the world. He is not bright, wonderful or powerful enough for us. Why does his strength not shine out more clearly? Why does he spare evil men and let men of good will be sacrificed? Why does he allow so much effort to be wasted? Why does he let so much half-finished work go to ruin and everything be begun again? Apparently he isn't a match for the world.

On the other hand, we should not forget that we are always inclined to be disappointed by what we have come to value and love most of all. The ultimate reality lacks the concentrated availability of what is in the foreground

of our experience. We can hardly expect what strikes us
as bright and wonderful to make the same impression on
everyone; this is often a painful experience. At the same
time, even the holiest people sometimes have doubts about
what or whom they love most of all—their wife, mother,
friend or God. But if we undertake the most important
task of all for the Christian, and try to overcome this
temptation to disappointment, we are bound to discover
that the ultimate reality cannot be demonstrated and that
it can appear only as our surrender of ourselves gets
closer to perfection. We cannot expect the object of our
love to be loved equally by all people. There is an ultimate point in man at which the gift is unique and
individual: something valid only for that one man.

Our attempt to overcome this temptation to be disappointed by God will gradually result in a deeper spiritual
experience of the world around us, and a disclosure of the
essential elements beneath the superficial features that
can be seen and understood by all men. This temptation
to be disappointed is undoubtedly a phase through which
we must all pass on our way towards the ultimate reality
of God.

The third temptation is that God directs us back to our
everyday lives. He did this by becoming a child and sub-
jecting himself to ordinary simple people. True religious-
ness and pride cannot co-exist in the same person. Man's
spirit is made more sensitive, more all-embracing and more
translucent when his experience of faith is authentic. The
limits of his own being are extended and a peak is reached
in his own existence which is at the same time a culminat-
ing point in the world. In spirit, he floats above a bright
abyss and the whole world seems, at times like this, to be

small and insignificant. His spirit transcends the world and enters a completely different and unknown sphere. A feeling of strength and greatness overcomes him.

But sooner or later the Christian has to return from this heightened experience and descend to the world of everyday life inhabited by ordinary, even miserable people —the world to which he is called by the God who became man, who became a little child. In this sense, Jesus's birth brought about a revolution in man's religious attitudes, making complete forgetfulness of one's own greatness and the overcoming of one's own pride the condition of true greatness. Since the Christ-event, greatness has only taken up its habitation in men who know that they are nothing and who have repudiated their own glory. Since Jesus's birth, there has been a close and indeed unbreakable connexion between the renunciation of greatness and true human greatness, in other words, between sacrifice and joy. What took place when a certain Jewish mother gave life to her child appears contradictory, because it is difficult to accept that sacrifice and joy can be one, that we can only enrich our lives by giving away and that we must renounce if we are to become really great. This contradiction is, after all, a truth that can never be proved—it can only be experienced.

The most powerful of all temptations that can assail the Christian is that the ultimate ground of the human reality can never be verified in this life. It is only if we endure this temptation until the end of our life that we can begin to understand that 'whoever exalts himself will be humbled, and whoever humbles himself will be exalted' (Matt. 23.12; Luke 14.11). It is almost impossible to express these extremely delicate aspects of the human heart in really fitting words. The Magnificat, the song of Mary which is the most appropriate of all Christmas songs, expresses this idea very beautifully: 'He has shown strength with his arm, he has scattered the proud in the imagination of their hearts, he has put down the mighty from their thrones, and exalted those of low degree; he has filled the hungry with good things, and the rich he has sent empty away' (Luke 1.51–3). Anyone who did not know where this song came from would perhaps think that it was a revolutionary song. In fact, it really is a song of the revolution—the revolution of Christmas.

The spirit of the incarnation can be expressed quite simply as: 'Though he was in the form of God, he did not count equality with God a thing to be grasped, but emptied himself, taking the form of a servant, being born in the likeness of men. And being found in human form he humbled himself and became obedient unto death, even death on a cross' (Phil. 2.6–8). This shows us that the prior condition of becoming a Christian is to empty oneself, to become completely selfless. Man finds his innermost reality by giving himself completely. By giving himself away, he at the same time preserves himself, completes himself and reaches fulfilment. He can only keep himself in this way, paradoxically, if he loosens his grip on himself. Human nature is essentially oriented towards an ecstasy—man must stand outside himself and reveal himself in order to find himself. The more he clings to himself, the less human he becomes.

The spirit of Jesus's incarnation is therefore the spirit of man's incarnation. If man locks himself up inside his own self, he will remain without promise. We may therefore say that, in the last resort, the process by which man becomes himself, his incarnation, includes death. (And this also applies to Jesus's incarnation, of course.) It is, more-over, in death that man is so completely taken away from himself that, if he gives his free consent to being taken away from himself in this way, he will be capable of be-ing completely humble; that is, that he will, by giving himself away completely, be able to fulfil his humanity. That is why Paul regards Jesus's incarnation as 'obedience unto death'. But in the mind of the Christian death im-mediately evokes the idea of resurrection: in the light of the incarnation, the way of the God who became a child is clearly revealed as the way of the God who died and rose again. The burden of Christmas is unutterably heavy, but its promise is very bright.

God created an entirely new order by becoming man: an order in which man can be completed and fulfilled by freely consenting to be small and insignificant. He has caught us up in a vital movement of self-detachment which, if we accept death, will lead to resurrection. To do that, he has had to overturn all our systems and all our ideas. He has had to expose us to the dangers involved in his being incalculable, disappointing us, and showing us the way back to everyday life; because only if we accept these dangers can we overcome our enclosure within our-selves and move towards our ultimate fulfilment.

One last point: Even if we have fully understood all this and taken in the message of Jesus's birth, we should not think for a moment that we have grasped the ultimate truth, or that the essence of it all has really taken hold of us. We have done no more than reach the end of one stage of our unending advance into the mystery. Our conception of it is simply the beginning of an even greater understanding. All that we do is to drive furiously after God, without ever catching him up or overtaking him. On our earthly level of existence this may seem very distressing; in fact it is the precondition for boundless happiness: the joy of seeking God.

*   *   *

The journey of the wise men from the East to Bethlehem symbolizes our existence here on earth and our ultimate fulfilment as human beings. We look for God, in order to find him, during our life on earth. We look for God, after we have found him, in eternal happiness.

So that men will continue to look for him in order to find him, God remains boundless, immeasurable, infinite. That is the structure of the creature's becoming God, a form of becoming that of its nature is never completed.

In this spirit, too, we kneel down in silence before the mystery of the God who became a little child. Perhaps, like the wise men from the East, we will be told to go back 'by another way' to our own country; in other words, back to the everyday world. Anyone who has once been seized by this God and has beheld his salvation has already begun a new life along entirely new ways.